THE CURSE OF THE WEREWOLF

A Play

KEN HILL

Songs by
IAN ARMIT and KEN HILL

SAMUEL FRENCH

LONDON
NEW YORK SYDNEY TORONTO HOLLYWOOD

THE CURSE OF THE WEREWOLF

Commissioned and first produced by the Contact Theatre Company, Manchester, on the 6th October 1976, with the following cast of characters (in the order of their appearance):

The Child	Philip Cragg or Angharad Cragg
The Pastor	Cliff Howells
The Gravedigger	David Mallinson
The Baron	Nicholas Geake
The Baroness	Binkie Shoebridge
1st Pallbearer	Richard Cragg
2nd Pallbearer	Ian Galley
D'Arcy	Benedict Campbell
Mrs Bancroft	Judith Barker
Dr Bancroft	Peter Dudley
Kitty	Joanna Mackie
Ramsey	Cliff Howells
Ingeborg	Binkie Shoebridge
✳ **Professor Konrad Steiner**	Christopher Ravenscroft
Attendant	Richard Cragg
✳ **Inspector Otto Krueger**	David Mallinson
✳ **Baron Martin von Heilmann**	Nicholas Geake
Hans	Cliff Howells
Lotty	Binkie Shoebridge
Ernst	Cliff Howells
Frau Gessler	Binkie Shoebridge
Sergeant	Cliff Howells

Directed by Kenneth Alan Taylor
Designed by Marty Flood
Lighting by Nick Jones
Dances arranged by Judith Barker
Musical direction, vocal and orchestral arrangements by Rodney Natkiel

The play is designed to be performed by nine actors, doubling as necessary.

THE CURSE OF THE WEREWOLF

STAGING

The setting consists of simple formalised levels, stairways and arches. The highest area is upstage centre and right, with a small door below it and central. To the right of this area is an entrance in the form of an arch, and beyond it upstage a larger arch looking out onto the sky. Cut invisibly into this area, stage right, is a grave-sized trap, with a lid hinged upstage. To the left of this area is a lower rostrum, two steps leading down to it, with an entrance in the form of an arch to the left, and beyond it upstage a larger arch looking out onto the sky. Below this area, and to the left, is an even lower rostrum which extends over the orchestra pit, or forestage, depending upon the design of the theatre, and into which, invisibly, is cut a smaller trap, as far downstage as possible. To the left of this area is an entrance in the form of an arch. The main downstage area is central and right, at stage level, reached by a step down from the latter rostrum. To the right of this area is an entrance in the form of an arch, and running around the area upstage centre and to the right, either side of entrances, is a low bench against the faces of the upstage rostrum and right wall. A similar short piece of bench is fixed against the left wall, downstage of the entrance. Above the entrance, against the left wall, is a short extension of the upstage left rostrum in the form of a table. Steps are provided down into the auditorium right, and the piano is set left of centre below the stage. In the background is a cyclorama and gauze, behind which is flown a moon box, and effects projectors.

AUTHOR'S NOTE

THE CURSE OF THE WEREWOLF is one of a series of plays which first saw the light of day at Theatre Workshop, Stratford East. And as one would expect, coming from such an illustrious source, it only works on a very truthful level. Any attempt to 'send it up' or 'guy' the performances will result in a very dull and unfunny evening's entertainment. The excitement and the laughter in the piece comes out of its genuine tension. It must be played in deadly earnest—one must *believe* in werewolves—one must believe in the people—and one must *care* what happens to them.

The pace of the play itself must be very fast, otherwise it will come out very long. The scenes should 'cut' into one another like a film, with furniture and props kept to the absolute minimum, and wherever possible set instantly by actors. On the other hand, all the action must be worked out very carefully, and time taken over it. When, for example, Kitty falls into a bog, we must believe this is *exactly* what is happening to her, and it should be many many nail-biting moments before we see that she is safe.

In the original production, a piano accompanied a great deal of the action, high-lighting tension, pointing out dramatic moments, underlaying the gentler, more romantic scenes. This is not essential, of course, but points in the script have been indicated for such a player. He should resist the temptation to 'quote' from well-known musical pieces. 'Land of Hope and Glory' may seem a funny idea to put behind Bancroft's determination to seek out and destroy the werewolf, but it will not be anywhere as effective as an invention of the pianist's own.

The play, in its present form, also contains nine songs*. They are very simple and easily sung, and provide a nice relief from the dark doings. However, for those companies who feel this is beyond them, they are quite easy to cut.

The setting described in this script is not that used in the original production, since it was felt that this would be beyond the resources of most amateur companies, whereas professional companies would in any case wish to design their own.

* The music for which is available from Samuel French Ltd.

MUSICAL NUMBERS

ACT I
Open Your Eyes   Kitty, Bancroft, D'Arcy, Mrs Bancroft, the
                               Company
Make A Little Wish   D'Arcy
Don't Sing The Words   Martin, Kitty, Mrs Bancroft, the Company
This Is The Start   Martin, Kitty
They're Ever So Evil   Martin

ACT II
Don't Be A Silly Sceptic   Otto, D'Arcy, Bancroft, the Company
I Like A Lot Of Friends   Kitty
Walpurgisdorf   Ingeborg
Lovers Can't Agree   D'Arcy
Reprise: Open Your Eyes   The Company

ACT 1

SCENE 1

(PROLOGUE)

Walpurgisdorf Church—1890

When the play begins, it is night. There is a large, pale moon, scudding clouds, and the faint sound of wind. All the players are heavily muffled against the cold in cloaks and overcoats of the period, and since in this scene they are speaking their native tongue, they do not have accents. The grave-trap is open, and the Gravedigger stands inside, digging. The piano plays sombre cortège music. At the sound of this, the Gravedigger looks off L, climbs out of the grave, and waits respectfully R of grave. A procession enters UL and crosses directly to the grave, climbing the steps. It is led by two pallbearers carrying a litter on which is the dead body of the Baroness, looking like Brunhilde on her shield. This is followed by the Old Baron. He carries a blunderbuss, and has his arm about a young boy, who has one arm in a sling. The litter is lowered to the ground above the grave-trap, and the pallbearers look questioningly towards the Old Baron. He gives a peremptory nod, and they bend to lift the litter into the grave. As they do so, a cry is heard off, DL

Pastor (*off*) Stop!

The Pastor runs on DL and hurries up the steps to the Old Baron's L

Stop, I say!

Baron Keep out of the way, Pastor.

Pastor I'm sorry, Baron, but I can't allow your wife to be buried here—not after what she's done! This is consecrated ground!

Baron And *this*, Pastor Schneidhuber, is a profane blunderbuss . . . ! (*He points the blunderbuss at the Pastor*) So stay away, or I'll blow your legs off!

The Pastor takes a step backwards, with what dignity he can muster

Pastor Since you insist.

The piano continues to underlay, as the Old Baron turns to the dead Baroness, bends over her, and kisses her. As he does so the long barking howl of a distant wolf is heard. All react, listening. As they do so, a black, shrouded figure appears below them, from DR, looking up at them, his back to us. The Baron catches sight of him and takes an involuntary step towards him

Baron You!

A*

For a moment, it seems he might raise his blunderbuss and shoot the man, but he restrains himself, turning quickly towards the Pastor

Read the service.

Pastor (*very definite*) Never. That I will never do. *Never.*

The Baron points the blunderbuss at him

Baron Read the service!

Pastor Oh well, just this once. (*He grumbles as he fumbles open a prayer-book*) I've heard of weddings, but a shotgun funeral is ridiculous ...

Baron (*in anguish*) Get on with it!

As the Pastor reads the pallbearers slowly lower the body into the grave

Pastor Oh Lord Jesus Christ, King of Glory, deliver the souls of the departed from the pains of Hell and from the deep pit: save them from the mouth of the lion, nor allow the dark lake to swallow them up, nor darkness to enshroud them ...

Faint wolf-howling is heard, and continues to the end of the prayer, gradually getting louder. The Pastor continues uneasily

With our prayers, O Lord, we offer up a sacrifice of praise: do Thou receive it on behalf of this soul whom we this day commit to Thy keeping. Grant O Lord that they may pass from death into life. Amen.

The howling is very loud. The Baron staggers towards the figure in black

Baron Damn you! Damn you!

The Baron tears at his throat and falls, tumbling off the edge of the rostrum to land DRC, close to the figure in black. The Gravedigger drops his spade, sits on the edge of the rostrum, and jumps down to examine him. The Young Boy comes forward to the extreme edge of the rostrum, looking down, wide-eyed. After his examination, the Gravedigger looks up at them in horror

Gravedigger He's dead.

The Gravedigger turns to look at the Man in Black. All look at him. He turns and goes silently, as he came, DR

Pastor And now this Church is defiled! Let no man set foot upon its desecrated soil again! ... Not for all time!

Loud wolf-howling. Wind rises to a crescendo and fades. Fade lighting to BLACKOUT. *The piano plays a thunderous passage, blending gradually into ragtime—a passage of time*

SCENE 2

Walpurgisdorf Castle—1922

The ragtime fades. Light returns. It is early evening, a sunset beginning to form through the US arches. A large ornate chair has been set R, not too far DS, and a small wooden door, studded with nails, is set in the small arch UC. The costumes must demonstrate strongly the period. D'Arcy is heard off, DL

D'Arcy (*off*) Hallo? Anybody at home?

He comes in DL. He is dressed as a butler, with a large overcoat covering the costume, and a hat. He is loaded down with skis, skates, baggage, etc.

Hallo? Is this the Schloss Walpurgisdorf? Hallo? (*He calls off behind him*) There's nobody here, Mrs Bancroft.

Mrs Bancroft comes on DL. She is a large formidable lady, dressed half in green silk and half in brown fur

Mrs Bancroft Hardly surprising. It was one of my husband's arrangements.

D'Arcy dumps what he is carrying on the upstage edge of the rostrum on which they are standing

And be careful of my skis, D'Arcy. They're hand-made hickory.

D'Arcy Sorry, Mrs Bancroft.

Mrs Bancroft crosses RC, stepping down to the lower level

Mrs Bancroft Look at this place. It's like a pigsty. They must have an English maid. (*Calling off DL*) Hugo! Come here at once!

Bancroft (*off*) Coming, my dear.

Mrs Bancroft Then hurry up!

Dr Bancroft comes on DL. He is a small man, dressed neatly, wearing a grey overcoat, hat and scarf

Bancroft I'm here, my dear.

Mrs Bancroft Which is more than your friend the Professor is. There's nobody here to greet us at all.

Bancroft That's odd. (*Crossing to her*) He must have got my cable.

Mrs Bancroft Why? *You* wrote and posted it, didn't you? It's probably on its way to Tipperary. (*She takes off her gloves, stuffs them into her hand-bag, and hangs it on the back of the chair*) And where's that daughter of yours, Hugo? Day-dreaming again, I suppose? (*Calling off DL*) Kitty! . . . Where on earth's the child got to?

D'Arcy I think she's looking at the view, Madam.

Mrs Bancroft View? What view? Just a lot of trees. (*She crosses to the chair and sits*) That's all I've seen for days now—trees, trees, trees. Nature simply has no imagination sometimes.

Bancroft Well, we *are* in the Bohemian Forest, my dear.

Mrs Bancroft I'm aware of that. I know what forests are made of. Just a lot of trees. But if it wasn't for this quixotic notion of yours for visiting an old Medical School chum, we could at least have gone to the *Black* Forest

D'Arcy Don't they have trees there?

Mrs Bancroft All the *best* people go to the Black Forest, D'Arcy. You wouldn't understand.

D'Arcy No, Madam. I'll go and fetch Miss Bancroft, shall I?
Mrs Bancroft No.

But she is too late—he has hurried out DL

And that's another thing, Hugo. We must keep an eye on that young man. We don't know nearly enough about him.
Bancroft D'Arcy? Seems a decent enough chap.
Mrs Bancroft His character's neither here nor there: he's a servant. I'm not sure, but I think I caught him using Kitty's christian name the other day.
Bancroft (*humouring her*) Good heavens! Did you really, dear?
Mrs Bancroft She's far too easy going, that daughter of yours. She didn't even kick him.
D'Arcy (*reappearing DL*) Here she is, Mrs Bancroft.

Kitty comes in, pretty and blonde, wearing white furs over a colourful dress. She runs across to her mother, and kneels beside her

Kitty Oh Mother, how can you bear it inside this gloomy old castle? It's so beautiful outside. There's a little old deserted church, high up on the mountain. Look—you can just see it through the gothic window. (*She rises and points off UL*)
Mrs Bancroft Through the trees, you mean.
Bancroft I don't think your mother likes it here, Kitty.
Mrs Bancroft I certainly do not. Especially those filthy peasants we passed. What did they think they were doing?
Kitty (*moving DC*) Just simple wood-cutters, Mother. Perfectly normal.
Mrs Bancroft Then why did that man cross himself when we asked the way here?
Bancroft I don't know. He seemed to be frightened of something. (*Eyeing his wife speculatively*) Can't imagine what.
D'Arcy (*moving down the steps to Kitty's L*) He certainly shot off into the woods quickly enough. All I said was Walpurgisdorf, and he was off like a whippet.
Mrs Bancroft Walpurgisdorf! What a name! What a place!
Kitty Honestly, Mother—you've no vision!

SONG: **Open Your Eyes**

Kitty	Oh all you have to do is open your eyes Look at the sun Look at the sky
Bancroft	Yes all you have to do is use your eyes Look at the clouds
Both	Give it a try . . . now
Both/D'Arcy	Oh all you have to do is just look around
Kitty	Isn't it fine?
Bancroft/D'Arcy	Isn't it fine?
Kitty	Isn't it grand?
Bancroft/D'Arcy	Isn't it grand?

All Three	Yes all you see is waiting there to be found
	Say that it's yours
	Hold out a hand . . . 'cause

By now, they have persuaded Mrs Bancroft to join in

Bancroft /D'Arcy	⎰Life ıs never quite as bad as you think it is
Kitty /Mrs B	⎱Ah . . . .

Kitty /Mrs B	Ski-da-di-dat!

Bancroft /D'Arcy	⎰Every day is just another—
Kitty /Mrs B	⎱Ah . . . .

All	—great adventure!

Kitty /Mrs B	But only if you always open your eyes
Kitty	Look at the blue
Bancroft /D'Arcy	Ooh ooh
Mrs B	Look at the green
Kitty	Boo-pi-doo, boo-pi-doo

All	Yes we must always open both of our eyes
	Take it all in
	See where we've been . . . to

Behind them, Ramsey appears, from UL, wearing a white coat, his hair standing on end. He looks at them in astonishment, and comes down the steps to their L, watching, during the following

All	(*fortissimo*) Now all you have to do is—
Ramsey	(*finger to lips, loud*) Ssssh!

Not seeing him, they take this as an instruction from one of themselves

All	(*pianissimo*) Look at the sun
Bancroft /D'Arcy	Ooh ooh
All	Look at the sky
Kitty /Mrs B	Boo-pi-doo, boo-pi-doo
	(*Gradual crescendo*)
Kitty	Look at the clouds
Bancroft /D'Arcy	Ooh ooh
Mrs Bancroft	Give it a try
Kitty	Boo-pi-doo, boo-pi-doo
Bancroft	Look at the blue
Kitty /Mrs B	Ooh ooh
D'Arcy	Look at the green
Kitty /Mrs B	Boo-pi-doo, boo-pi-doo
All	Take it all in
	Ooh ooh
	See where you've been
	Boo-pi-doo, boo-pi-doo!

At the end of the song, Ramsey applauds. They turn and look at him

Mrs Bancroft Hugo! What have you made me do? Your host is here!
Bancroft What? Where? (*Seeing Ramsey*) Oh, but good heavens—
Ramsey Don't mind me. I quite like it. I'm musical myself.

He moves down the steps towards them, taking C. D'Arcy and Kitty break upstage. He takes a penny whistle from his pocket and plays it. This, and further cues, can be doubled by the piano in the treble, if the actor cannot play the whistle

Mrs Bancroft What's he doing?
Bancroft I've no idea, my dear. But you see, that's not—
Mrs Bancroft (*to Ramsey*) What are you doing, man?
Ramsey Now that's a very good question. (*He crosses to her, below Bancroft*) Most people can tell. Most people take one look at me and say 'You're playing the penny whistle' or 'Why are you playing that penny whistle?' You're the first person who simply said 'What are you doing?' Because, you see, I don't know. These other people, they only *thought* I was playing the penny whistle. Actually, I wasn't. I can't *play* the penny whistle.
Mrs Bancroft (*her head spinning*) Then you're not musical?
Ramsey I certainly am. I'm perhaps the most complete musician the world's ever known. I can't play a note.
D'Arcy (*coming down LC*) Isn't that a drawback?

Ramsey turns on him

Bancroft Excuse me, my dear—
Mrs Bancroft Quiet, Hugo.
Ramsey (*to D'Arcy*) Now that's another good question. It shows you've been listening to me. A lot of people don't. What I mean is, I can't play the notes everybody else plays. I play notes of my own. They're better.
Kitty (*moving down to his L*) How?
Ramsey They sound better.
Mrs Bancroft Who says?
Ramsey I say.
D'Arcy What does everybody else say?
Ramsey I haven't asked them.
Kitty Why not?
Ramsey They never listen to me. Every time I try to play, they go away.
Mrs Bancroft Where to?
Ramsey Oh not far—just out of earshot. But you appreciate the problem?
D'Arcy Definitely.
Ramsey (*crossing L and up the steps*) I'm perhaps the greatest musician Barrow-in-Furness has ever produced, only I can't prove it. It's quite driving me sane. (*He suddenly lifts up his head and howls like a wolf. All stare at him transfixed. He coughs apologetically*) I beg your pardon— a touch of lycanthropy.

Minor chords from piano. They all begin to edge R, away from him

All Oh—that's quite all right.

Ramsey It was all Janet's fault. She wouldn't give me what I needed, so I had to sublimate into my whistle.

Mrs Bancroft Did you now?

Kitty Who's Janet?

Ramsey My mother. Everybody said it wouldn't last. (*He howls like a wolf, and begins to prance, snarling and laughing maniacally*) I'm a wolf, I'm a wolf! Had you all fooled! I'm not a musician at all! That was just a ruse! Now I'm going to eat you all up!

There is a sudden loud crash, off, UL, and Ingeborg comes on—very large, with blonde plaits, wearing a white coat. She is followed by two attendants, in white coats

Ingeborg Vorsicht! Packt ihn! Schnell! Schnell!

The two attendants hurry down the steps to Ramsey, grab hold of him, and begin to subdue him. He fights back, howling and snarling. Mrs Bancroft crosses to C, below Bancroft, staring at this

Mrs Bancroft Good heavens, Hugo, your friend's a raving maniac.

Bancroft But I've been trying to tell you, my dear. *That* isn't *him*.

Steiner appears very suddenly, behind him, lit from behind—a tall, gaunt figure, dressed in black, with a little beard, toying with a monocle. His German accent is soft and sinister

Steiner No.

All jump, turn to look at him

He is a patient of mine. (*He crosses below them, his eyes on Ramsey*)

Bancroft Ah Konrad, good to see you—

Steiner (*not looking at him*) Quiet! . . . (*He speaks gently to the struggling Ramsey*) Now Ramsey, calm yourself, my friend. Why, it's dinner time.

Ramsey Dinner time!

Steiner Yes, we have a rabbit for you.

Ramsey (*in ecstasy*) Rabbit! . . . Oh, *rabbit*!

D'Arcy (*breathless*) Does he like rabbit stew, then?

Steiner No. (*He produces a wriggling white rabbit from his pocket, held by the ears. Although a dummy, he should cause it to wriggle and look as real as possible*) Come on, Ramsey. That's right. There's a good fellow. Come this way.

He coaxes Ramsey over R, still held by the two attendants. The others break DC, watching in amazement. Ramsey turns on them suddenly

Ramsey Get away from here! It's dangerous! Get away while you can!

Steiner (*to the attendants, sharply*) Raus mit ihm!

Ramsey I mean it! Get away! As far as you can!

Steiner Schnell!

They drag him out. Dr Steiner throws the rabbit out after them, then turns and speaks up to Ingeborg

Ingeborg, du bleibst hier.
Ingeborg Jawohl.
Kitty What did he mean by all that?

Steiner is instantly smitten by her, and crosses to her

Steiner (*smiling brilliantly*) Nothing, my dear. Please don't concern yourself. He is raving, that is all. (*He kisses her hand*)
Bancroft Erm—this is my daughter, Kitty.
Steiner Charmed. More than charmed. (*He refuses to let the hand go*)
Bancroft And Eunice, my wife. This is Professor Steiner, my dear. You know—my old school chum.
D'Arcy (*not liking the way Steiner is hanging onto Kitty's hand*) And I'm D'Arcy.
Mrs Bancroft The butler. Shut up, D'Arcy. Nobody wants to know who you are.

Steiner finally releases Kitty's hand

Steiner Ingeborg.
Ingeborg Zu befehl?
Steiner Bring unsere Gäster was zu Trinken.
Ingeborg Jawohl, Herr Professor.

She crosses behind them and goes off UC, below the rostrum

Bancroft Look here, Konrad, don't you think it's a bit dangerous—letting chaps like that roam around loose?
Steiner You need have no fear, Bancroft. Ramsey is quite harmless. Besides, if we locked up everybody around here who thought he was a wolf, we should be bursting at the seams. It's a local malady.
Mrs Bancroft Not only local, Professor. That idiot came from Barrow-in-Furness—though God forbid anybody should. He was English.
Steiner (*turning away from her L*) Well . . . I'm rather well-known for my treatment of lycanthropy.

Minor chords from the piano as he ascends the steps to L

Admirers of mine sometimes send me patients from abroad.
D'Arcy (*not liking him at all*) Rather like a Christmas present, what?
Steiner (*turning on him, the feeling mutual*) Exactly like.

Ingeborg returns from C, carrying a small tray with three drinks on it. She comes down C between Bancroft and Kitty and offers drinks, first to Mrs Bancroft and Bancroft, and then to Kitty

But tell me, my dear Bancroft, your presence here is something of a surprise. Where is the car I sent you? Were you not collected at the rail-head?
Mrs Bancroft (*sitting in the chair*) Not us. We had to trudge for miles through that blessed tree-filled forest.

Steiner (*in horror*) You *walked*?

Minor chords. He and Ingeborg exchange looks

Mrs Bancroft It's all right—*D'Arcy* carried the luggage.

Steiner Madam, it is extremely dangerous to walk alone in the forest. I must warn you that it is the wolf season here.

Loud howling, off

Kitty (*whispering*) Is that one now?

Steiner No it's just Ramsey eating his rabbit.

Maniacal laughter, off

Mrs Bancroft Not very homely, is it? How do you sleep nights?

Steiner (*wandering to R of the chair*) Oh, we manage. In fact, we find it rather restful—don't we, Ingeborg? (*He turns to her*)

Ingeborg (*smiling hugely*) Bestimmt, Herr Professor. (*She turns and takes the tray off*)

Bancroft You always were a queer fish, Konrad. Hardly surprising you took up this line of work, what?

Steiner My dear Bancroft, I became a psychoanalyst because it was a challenge—a far greater challenge than the banal complaints of the flesh that fill *your* working day.

Bancroft Well, at least I treat my patients. At least, they get *better*.

Mrs Bancroft Some of them.

Bancroft You can't show me that psychoanalysis has ever cured anybody of anything.

Steiner Perhaps not. But a psychoanalyst is more than a mere doctor ... to *work* with madmen ... to *be* with them ...

Music underlays gently as he talks, crossing up the steps to the second level. During the speech, Ingeborg returns and comes slowly to Mrs Bancroft, listening

To live their fantasies ... to journey deep into the schizophrenic dungeons of their minds ... to taste their unnatural lusts and their hideous dreams ... One needs to be an artist ... one needs to be a poet ... for madness is *beautiful* ...

The music dies

Bancroft (*a little embarrassed*) Quite.

During the speech, the lighting has dimmed a little, and now the dark figure of Otto appears in the archway UL, behind Steiner. He is a sinister figure in black police uniform, and leather coat, pistol in a belted holster. One hand is covered in a black glove, and carries the other. Kitty sees him and screams. Steiner turns on him sharply

Ingeborg Donner und Blitze, Herr Professor! Sehen Sie mal!

Otto comes forward, pausing at the steps above Steiner

Steiner Was machen Sie denn da? (*To the others*) Forgive me. Our Chief of Police sometimes thinks he can go wherever he pleases. I'm sure he didn't mean to startle you.

Otto comes down the steps to Steiner

Otto I was passing. The windows were open.
Steiner And the conversation was carrying. Quite. These are my guests I told you about—the Bancrofts.

Otto steps down towards them, and Bancroft comes to meet him

Bancroft How do you do?

Bancroft holds out his hand. Otto clicks his heels and salutes with his black-gloved hand. He seems to have a lot of trouble making it work

Otto May I enquire whether you have reported to my sergeant yet?
Bancroft Well, no, we've only just—
Otto All visitors must present their passports for inspection on arrival. It is the law.
Bancroft I'm sorry. I do beg your pardon. We'll do it first thing in the morning. Will that be satisfactory?
Otto No. But I will suffer it this once. (*He turns to Steiner*) Wo ist der Baron?
Steiner Warum fragen Sie mich sowas? Ich bin nicht für ihn verantwortlich. Warum suchen Sie ihn nicht selbst?
Otto Das mache ich.

He turns and ascends the steps above Steiner, ready to leave the way he came in. As he does so, however, he drops his black glove. He turns and looks down at it. Kitty bends, picks it up, and hands it to him. He has to force his hand to work to take it from her

Danke schön.

He strides out

Kitty What an extraordinary man? What's wrong with his hand?
Steiner He lost it as a child. And now I really must belatedly play the host. Ingeborg, show the ladies to their rooms. Bancroft, will you come with me.

Mrs Bancroft rises. Bancroft follows Steiner up the steps

D'Arcy What about me?
Steiner Don't worry. We'll find something suitable for you.
D'Arcy I'm not sleeping in a stables again. Those blasted horses kept me awake last night.
Mrs Bancroft Stop complaining, D'Arcy. Just wait here and behave yourself. Come along, Kitty.
Kitty In a moment, Mummy. I want to watch the sunset.
Mrs Bancroft All right, dear—so long as you're not too late.

By now, Steiner has led Bancroft up the left hand stairs L, and has turned up the centre stairs, ready to cross and leave. Ingeborg is waiting to take Mrs Bancroft out DR

Kitty Tell me, Professor, that little old church up on the mountainside . . .

Minor chords from the piano. Ingeborg turns and looks up at Steiner. He pauses and looks sharply down at her

Steiner Yes?
Kitty Does anybody live up there now?
Steiner No. Nobody even goes there any more. It is deserted.

He goes out with Bancroft. Ingeborg and Mrs Bancroft go out. Kitty moves to lean against the high rostrum, looking off through the arch. The light is dying, the sky growing redder

D'Arcy Miss Bancroft . . .
Kitty (*dreamily*) Yes, D'Arcy?
D'Arcy Oh, Miss Bancroft . . .
Kitty (*suddenly*) It's gone all red.
D'Arcy (*startled*) What has?
Kitty The sky. It's quite beautiful.
D'Arcy Not half so beautiful as you, Miss Bancroft! You are more than sunset to me—you are the sun itself!
Kitty (*turning to him, dreamily*) What was that again, D'Arcy? I'm so sorry—I wasn't listening.
D'Arcy Oh, Miss Bancroft, if only you knew how lucky I feel!
Kitty Why?
D'Arcy Because that other butler broke his leg, ski-ing with you in the Alps.
Kitty It was his own fault. He should have got out of Mother's way.
D'Arcy (*turning to her*) Yes, but *I* happened to be there! . . . A penniless vagabond . . . only too willing to take on the job at short notice . . . Tell me, Miss Bancroft, does my pennilessness cause you concern?
Kitty (*turning and looking at him in surprise*) Not in the slightest. Why should it?
D'Arcy (*going to her quickly and holding her hands*) Oh Miss Bancroft, you make me so happy!
Kitty (*disengaging herself*) Careful, D'Arcy. Remember where you are. We don't want to upset Mummy, do we now? (*She moves to the arch*)
D'Arcy Then I'm wasting my time?
Kitty (*turning and smiling at him*) I didn't say that. Let's just wait and see, shall we?

She goes out. D'Arcy moves quickly DC and speaks to the audience

D'Arcy Dare I tell her the truth? This penniless façade discountenances me at times. But no! I want her to love me for myself alone—not as the rich Lord D'Arcy of Faversham! . . . And I won't give up. No, I'm going

to stick this thing out to the end! After all *anything's* possible! All you have to do is—

SONG: **Make A Little Wish**

D'Arcy   Make a little wish
And maybe some day
There will come a dream
That turns out your way
All you got to do is suppose
That anything goes

Make a little wish
Whatever some say
Foolish though it seem
Just try it one day
All you got to do is propose
That anything goes

Luck's got a purpose behind it
Fortune is more than a name
Luck is for those that can find it
No matter what the state of the game

Make a little wish
And then believe it
Don't you ever doubt
That you'll achieve it
All you got to say is, Who knows?
Well, anything goes

(*He dances time-steps through the next verse and middle eight*)

Make a little wish
And maybe some day
There will come a dream
That turns out your way
All you got to do is suppose
That anything goes
Believe it
All you got to do is suppose
That anything goes

Mrs Bancroft (*off*) D'Arcy! Come here at once!
D'Arcy Yes, Mrs bloody Bancroft.

He grabs up cases, skis, skates quickly, and hurries off. Fade to BLACKOUT

1st Cleveys ·
Pafinier ·

SCENE 3

Kitty's Bedroom

During the BLACKOUT, *a chiming clock is heard, and Kitty's bed, with Kitty in it, is trucked on swiftly and silently from UR onto the high UR rostrum, as far L as possible, parallel with the audience, and her head to the L. A gauze net is flown or drawn over the UR arch. Pale moonlight then lights the area. The moon box is lit and visible through the gauze. Kitty turns restlessly in bed, then quietens. Minor chords from the piano. The creak of an opening door, and Ramsey creeps in from UR. He crosses quietly above the bed, looking down at her. As he looks down at her another creak is heard and he ducks down out of sight. Ingeborg creeps in, goes to the bed, crossing below it, and gently draws the coverlet down, baring Kitty's throat and shoulders. She gives a nasty smile, then creeps out. Ramsey's head appears above the bed, then he rises, fumbles in his pocket. As he does so, another creak is heard and he ducks down again. Steiner creeps in. He crosses below the bed, and looks down at Kitty, a malignant smile on his face*

Steiner (*nodding to himself and whispering*) Yes . . . (*He takes a stethoscope from his pocket and applies it to Kitty's breast. He nods, smiles and whispers again*) Yes . . .

A faint, distant, wolf-howl is heard. Steiner crosses around the bed R, and goes to the arch, peering through the gauze. He turns and looks back at Kitty, smiling and whispering once more

Yes . . .

He turns to go off. As he does so, the invisible Ramsey sneezes. Steiner pauses and looks back suspiciously. A brief pause, and then he goes R. A further brief pause, and then Ramsey's head appears, looking off after Steiner. He rises, fumbles in his pocket, takes out the whistle and places it gently under Kitty's pillow. He then turns and creeps off UR. A faint wolf-howl is heard and Kitty sits up suddenly in bed

Kitty What's that? Who's there? (*She looks around*) For a moment, I thought there was somebody in my room. (*She goes to settle down again, and the whistle is heard to fall to the floor*) What on earth . . . ? (*She picks it up*) How did that get here? (*She looks around once more, examines it curiously, then experimentally gives it a little blow. The sound she makes startles her at first, but then—warming to the idea—she begins playing it. As she does so, build in ominous minor chords from the piano. A dark figure slowly becomes visible through the gauze. Kitty sees it, gasps, and stops playing*) Who's there? (*Silence. She gets out of bed, and pulls on a negligé which is thrown over the head of the bed*) Who is it?

Silence. Very cautiously, she goes slowly to the window, reaches out for the gauze curtains, and then—suddenly—draws them open. Martin von Heilmann takes a step forward and smiles at her, She recoils to the edge of the rostrum with a little cry. Martin is dressed in a fur-lined coat, a fur hat on his head. He has enormous continental charm, and immediately puts her at her ease

Martin Forgive me. I didn't mean to startle you. I was walking outside on the terrace, when I heard you playing.

Kitty On the terrace? . . . Playing?

Martin indicates the whistle she still has clutched in her hand. It embarrasses her

Oh yes, this. I'm sorry, I don't know why. (*She crosses quickly to below the bed*) I don't even know where it came from. (*She puts it down on the pillow of the bed*)

Martin I thought it charming. I was intrigued. I stepped over the balustrade to listen. It seemed very natural at the time.

Kitty But . . . but . . . who are you?

Martin (*clicking his heels and bowing*) Martin von Heilmann at your service, Miss Bancroft.

Kitty You know me?

Martin (*moving a little into the room*) Oh yes. I saw you arrive.

Kitty Then you're from the village?

Martin In a manner of speaking.

Kitty (*recovering her composure*) Well, I don't think you'd better let the Professor find you here. He doesn't strike me as the sort of man who'd take kindly to trespassers.

Martin The reward is worth the risk.

Kitty Reward?

Martin Seeing you close to like this. You're even more beautiful than I thought.

Kitty (*flustered, and patting her hair*) Oh, do you think so? I'm sure I look a mess really. I don't know why I got up. Something must have woken me.

Martin (*turning and moving a little back to the arch*) The wolves, I expect. They come very close this time of the year.

Kitty Oh, how awful! (*She kneels on the bed, facing him*) And you're out there all on your own. Don't they frighten you?

Martin (*turning to her, amused*) Frighten *me*? Why no, they don't frighten me. What an amusing idea.

Pause

Kitty It's very dark, isn't it?

Martin Yes, the clouds are covering the moon. It's unfortunate.

Minor chords

Kitty Why?

Martin We can't see one another properly. That's unfortunate, don't you think?

Pause

But forgive me, I'm keeping you up and you're cold. I'll leave you.

He turns to go towards the arch. Kitty jumps off the bed, upstage, and meets him

Kitty Will I . . . will I . . . see you again?

Martin Possibly. In fact, certainly. Yes, I shall see you tomorrow evening—down by the lake.

Kitty Tomorrow evening?

Martin Yes, the whole village will be there. Skating. It is a kind of festival. You do skate, do you not?

Kitty Oh yes, of course I do.

Martin Then we shall meet again. (*He takes her hand, bows his head, clicks his heels*) Auf wiederseh'n, Fräulein.

He goes off quickly through the arch, turning R

Kitty Goodnight!

Martin (*off*) Goodnight!

Kitty (*turning to the front, quite thrilled with the encounter*) Oh, how ripping!

She flings off her negligé and jumps happily into bed. Fade quickly to BLACKOUT

2nd change

SCENE 4

The Lake

Immediately on the BLACKOUT, *there is loud waltz music played on the piano. The bed is trucked swiftly off, the small door UC folded back out of sight, and a small rustic table and chair are set DL on the low rostrum, near the step. Full, bright lighting reveals Steiner sitting at the table, dressed in overcoat, with fur hat and mittens, sipping a stein. The lower level, R and C is being used as the frozen surface of the lake, where D'Arcy, Bancroft, Mrs Bancroft, Lotty and Hans are skating. The skating is a simple mime on the floor of the stage, and all wear slip-on silver overshoes to suggest the skates. D'Arcy skates alone— quite competently—hands behind back, a long scarf around his neck. Bancroft is doing his best to support Mrs Bancroft, who sprawls all over the place—both wrapped up well against the cold. Hans and Lotty are two local villagers in colourful costume, who skate together. The quicker the 'cut' from the last scene to this, the better. Certainly the music and ad lib chatter should happen immediately, even if we are still in a* BLACKOUT. *The music continues to underlay the dialogue and skating, at a lower level*

Mrs Bancroft Oh do be careful, Hugo! I could have been damaged!

Bancroft Not while I'm here to break your fall, my dear. (*Calling to D'Arcy*) D'Arcy!

D'Arcy (*skating closer*) Did you call, sir?

Bancroft Yes. You're better at this game than I am. Skate with your mistress.

D'Arcy (*who is really waiting for Kitty to show up*) Oh but sir, actually I'm—(*indicates DR entrance*)

Mrs Bancroft Stop quibbling, D'Arcy. There's nothing to it. I'm quite proficient.

Mrs Bancroft throws her arms around D'Arcy's neck, and he supports her. Bancroft skates L to be near Steiner, and sits on the step by him, his feet still on the 'ice'

Steiner (*cynically*) It will never cease to amaze me how easily you English are amused.

Bancroft I wish I could say the same for the Germans. But you know, Konrad, you've changed. You're not the young man I remember.

Steiner And what young fellow was that?

Bancroft Why, the old chum who put a freshly-removed appendix into the Dean's boot—the wag who slipped a cadaver into Matron's bath water! ... (*Shaking his head, reminiscing*) Happy days! ... (*More seriously*) But now, you see, you've changed. You've become much more serious.

Steiner That's easily explained, Bancroft. I've grown up—a thing that happens everywhere in the world except England, I think. I've found my life's work. I think of nothing else. My work is unique.

Bancroft There are plenty of other psychoanalysts.

Steiner (*with great meaning*) Not like me. (*Laughing oddly*) Not like me.

The music swells, and the chatter builds on the ice

Mrs Bancroft Take my *weight*, D'Arcy!

D'Arcy I've got it, Mrs Bancroft. I'd just like to give it back if I can.

Kitty appears in DR entrance, dressed in short, fur-trimmed skirt, white boots, white fur hat

Kitty Hallo, everybody!

D'Arcy Oh, there you are, Miss Bancroft. Do hurry up. It's rather fun. I'll show you how.

Kitty I *know* how, thank you, D'Arcy.

She glides forward prettily and proceeds to skate rings round them. Hans and Lotty are very impressed, and cry out delightedly. Otto appears UR on the high rostrum, glaring down at them. At the sound of his voice, the happy music ceases

Otto (*shouting down*) Vorsicht! Das Eis ist zu dünn—dort sollte man nicht schlittschuhlaufen!

He crosses quickly down the steps. Hans and Lotty stop, and skate to sit on the bench, their feet still on the 'ice'. Kitty, D'Arcy and Mrs Bancroft stop and stare at him

Bancroft What's he say?

Steiner He says the ice is too thin for skating. It's nonsense, of course.

Otto comes down the second set of steps to Steiner's L, still shouting at the skaters

Otto Übrigens, Sie haben keine Erlaubnis bekommen!
Steiner And besides, they haven't asked his permission.

Otto takes papers from his pocket and glares down at Bancroft

Otto Your papers are not in order.
Bancroft (*startled*) What?
Otto (*indicating each one*) The passport is made out in the name of Hugo
    Matthew Bancroft, the visa is in the name of H. M. Bancroft, and your
    travel documents are in the name of Doctor Bancroft. It is most irregular.
Bancroft (*joking*) You're not going to put me in prison, are you?
Otto (*no sense of humour*) No. You are a guest of the Herr Professor's.
    But I warn you that your career of crime cannot continue indefinitely.

> *A sudden arpeggio on the piano and Martin runs on DR, leaps high in
> the air, and lands in the middle of the skaters. Cries of delight from Hans
> and Lotty who rise again*

Martin (*to Kitty*) We meet again!
Kitty I thought you were never coming.
Martin A von Heilmann always keeps his word—especially to a pretty
    lady. Permit me.

*He skates with her. The music breaks out again. They perform splendidly
and acrobatically, Martin lifting and holding Kitty, each movement punctu-
ated with cries of approval from Hans and Lotty*

D'Arcy (*jealously trying to leave Mrs Bancroft*) Excuse me, Mrs Bancroft,
    I'll just—
Mrs Bancroft Don't let go of me, D'Arcy!
D'Arcy Don't you think it's time I gave your daughter a twirl?
Mrs Bancroft Certainly not!
Bancroft (*to Steiner*) I say, that chap's rather good, isn't he?
D'Arcy (*overhearing, sourly*) Show off. Anybody can do that.

Kitty and Martin come to the end of a difficult routine

Mrs Bancroft (*calling to Martin*) Young man, I'd really rather you didn't
    throw my daughter around like that, if you don't mind.

Martin yodels, grinning at her, ignoring the command, skating with Kitty

(*to Bancroft*) Hugo! Say something!
Bancroft She won't take any notice of me, my dear. I'm only her father.
Steiner (*calling across to Martin*) Martin, fass das Mädchen nicht so an—
    Ihre Eltern machen sich Sorgen.

Martin laughs, ignoring him also, still dancing with Kitty

Otto (*shouting*) Tun Sie, was er Ihnen sagt! Es ist gefährlich. Das Eis ist
    zu dünn!

*Martin glares at him, stops dancing, jerks his head at Hans and Lotty. They
skate off, DR. Martin bounces on the ice, testing it. The music ceases. By now,*

D'Arcy and Mrs Bancroft are C, Mrs Bancroft L of D'Arcy near Bancroft.
Kitty and Martin are RC, Kitty on Martin's R

Mrs Bancroft I don't know how one behaves in your neck of the woods,
young man, but where *I* come from, we are introduced before we break
one another's arms and legs.

Kitty Mother! Martin was only skating with me—(*holding onto his arm
adoringly*) and rather splendidly too.

D'Arcy (*sourly*) I've seen better.

Mrs Bancroft Martin? (*Glaring at Kitty suspiciously*) How do you know
his Christian name? You've only just met.

Kitty looks uncomfortably up at Martin

Have you been slipping away while my back's been turned?

Kitty No, Mother.

Mrs Bancroft (*turning angrily to Bancroft*) Hugo, say something!

*Bancroft opens his mouth and lifts a finger, but Mrs Bancroft swings back on
Kitty and ploughs on*

Kitty, you're a complete disgrace to us sometimes! (*She swings on
Bancroft*) Hugo, *say* something to her!

Bancroft (*lifting a finger*) Now, Kitty—

Mrs Bancroft (*ignoring him, to Kitty*) That incident in Vienna was bad
enough! (*She swings on Bancroft*) Hugo, for goodness sake, are you just
going to *sit* there? You *never* speak harshly to the child!

Bancroft Shan't tell you again, K—

Mrs Bancroft (*ignoring him, to Kitty*) Kitty, there are things we do,
and there are things we do not. I thought you knew that. (*She swings
on Bancroft*) For heaven's sake, Hugo, will you *say* something! Behave
like a father for once!

Bancroft I certainly shall, my dear. (*Pause*) What do you want me to say?

Martin (*apologetically*) I'm afraid it's all my fault, Mrs Bancroft. You see,
I bumped into your daughter last night—on the terrace outside her
room.

Mrs Bancroft Then you were trespassing. (*To Otto, indicating Martin*)
Arrest this man!

Kitty (*despairingly*) Oh Martin, you needn't have said anything. I wouldn't
have told.

D'Arcy (*angrily*) Now look here—(*He takes a pace forward, and slips on
the ice. He crawls to his feet during the following*)

Mrs Bancroft (*to Otto*) Well, Inspector? He's admitted accosting my
daughter on private property. Isn't that a crime in this godforsaken
country?

Otto Not when the person concerned *owns* the property, Madam.

Mrs Bancroft (*startled*) What?

Steiner I'm afraid he's right, Mrs Bancroft. Martin owns not only the
castle, the village and the surrounding woods, but also the very lake on
which you have just now been skating. *You* are the trespassers, not he.

Mrs Bancroft *completely flustered*) I—

Bancroft (*rising*) I think, Konrad. you had better introduce us.

Steiner By all means. Doctor and Mrs Bancroft, Miss Bancroft, the Baron Martin von Heilmann.

Mrs Bancroft (*impressed*) *Baron*? Did you say *Baron*? (*To Martin*) Aren't you rather young to be a Baron?

Martin (*roguishly*) Aren't *you* rather young to be Kitty's mother? (*He kisses her hand to her great delight*)

Kitty (*breaking DR a little, adoringly*) A Baron! Oh, how wonderful!

D'Arcy (*fed up*) What's so special about a Baron? I'm . . . on very intimate terms with a Lord.

Mrs Bancroft Oh, shut up, D'Arcy.

Bancroft All the same, sir, I should like to know what you thought you were doing outside my daughter's room last night?

Martin I was listening. She called to me like a Siren.

Bancroft What are you talking about?

Kitty This, Daddy. (*She produces the whistle*) I found it in my bedroom.

Heavy minor chords. Steiner rises, comes quickly round the table and down on to the step

Steiner Let me see that, please.

Kitty skates across and gives it to him

   Where did you find this?

Kitty I told you. It was in my room.

Bancroft (*peering over Steiner's shoulder*) Is it important?

Steiner turns to find Otto's eyes on him, and speaks excessively casually

Steiner No, no, it belongs to one of my patients. I shall return it to him in the morning.

Steiner crosses back to his chair, not sitting for a moment, as if in thought. Martin skates down to Kitty's R and puts an arm round her

Martin And now I insist you shall all be my guests. (*Imperiously, to D'Arcy*) You, go and fetch some warm wine. Tell the innkeeper it is for the Baron. Schnell!

D'Arcy (*sarcastically saluting*) Jawohl, mein Kapitän!

D'Arcy crosses to the steps above Bancroft, sits a moment to take his overshoes off, and then goes out. Steiner sits again

Martin I trust you are all quite comfortable in my simple abode?

Mrs Bancroft Hardly simple, Baron. I think I counted sixteen bedrooms.

Martin Well, we used to be a very large family. (*He roars with laughter, digging her in the ribs. She enjoys it, but Bancroft finds himself vaguely disliking the man*)

Bancroft Used to be? Not any more?

Martin No, I'm afraid not. I am the last of the von Heilmanns. (*Glancing* *wickedly at Kitty*) Unless I preserve my line. (*He winks at Mrs Bancroft, who shrieks with laughter*)

Kitty Tell me something, Martin, if you own everything, do you also own that little church up on the mountain?

Minor chords. Otto starts. Martin and Steiner exchange glances. Music underlays the following

Martin Why do you ask?

Kitty I just wondered. It looks so fascinating. Do you?

Martin Yes. It has been in my family for generations. We are all buried there.

Kitty Perhaps I could look around it one day.

Martin Perhaps.

Otto You will have to go there alone. No villager will guide you.

Bancroft (*turning to him*) Why not?

Otto Because . . . it is haunted.

Steiner (*disgusted, hardly audible*) Arschloch!

Otto I have seen the ghost myself. It is an old man, dressed as a priest . . . with staring eyes . . . He glides through the very walls . . . his hands outstretched . . . reaching for your *neck*! . . . (*His black-gloved hand grabs his own neck, and locks. He wrestles with it, forcing it to open just in time*)

Kitty (*breathless*) And then?

Otto Then nothing. You see no more. You are too busy running away.

The musical underlay ceases. There is a pause

Martin (*cheering them all up*) Oh, but this is ridiculous, wasting our time talking about ghosts! . . . Mrs Bancroft, Kitty—won't you join me in a little exercise?

Mrs Bancroft We should be delighted, Baron.

Martin Everybody! On the ice, while there is still some daylight left! You too, Konrad! And you, Otto! There are spare skates! It is my request!

Reluctantly, Steiner and Otto pull on overshoes as D'Arcy returns quickly from DL, carrying a tray of steaming mugs

D'Arcy Your warm wine, sir. Sorry it took so long, but I made the mistake of telling them who it was for.

Martin (*impatient with him*) Never mind all that. Put it down over there, and see it doesn't get cold.

D'Arcy puts the tray on the table, and—seeing what is planned—sits quickly on the steps above it, and pulls on his overshoes. Martin puts an arm each around Kitty and Mrs Bancroft

Mrs Bancroft Not so close, please, Baron. It's scarcely proper.

Martin Proper? What is proper? Merely a word, my dear Madam.

SONG: Don't Sing The Words

During the course of this song, they skate, forming patterns, lines, etc. The chorus is intended to be yodelled, but this is difficult, and unless anybody can do so it should be la-la-ed as indicated

Martin
Don't sing the words
They just come between us
They don't seem to mean as much as
Tra la la la la

Martin /Kitty /
Mrs Bancroft
Study the birds
They just sing for pleasure
They don't try to measure
Tra la la la la la

All
(*clapping*)
Tra la la la la la la la la la la la
Tra la la la la la la la la la la la
Tra la la la la la la la la la la la
Tra la la la la la la la la la la la

Kitty
Don't sing the words
They don't show the way for us
They don't seem to say as much as

All
Tra la la la la

Kitty /Martin
Study the birds
They just sing for leisure
It's all that they treasure

All
Tra la la la la la

All
(*clapping*)
Tra la la la la la la la la la la la
Tra la la la la la la la la la la la
Tra la la la la la la la la la la la
Tra la la la la la la la la la la la

One orchestral verse now, in which the full company, led by Martin, Steiner and Otto perform a complicated, concerted, hand-thigh-and-foot-slapping routine

Don't sing the words
They just come between us
They don't seem to mean as much as
Tra la la la la
Study the birds
They just sing for pleasure
They don't try to measure
Tra la la la la la

At the end of the song, a woman's terrible scream, off, and Frau Gessler staggers in from the arch, UL. There are bloody rags about one wrist. The lighting fades a little

Kitty It sounded like a scream!
Mrs Bancroft (*pointing*) Look!

Frau Gessler staggers down the steps to DL

Otto It's Frau Gessler!
Bancroft She's hurt!

She collapses into Steiner's table, crashing to the ground. Otto and Steiner kick off their overshoes and hurry to her, Steiner to her L, Otto above her. Bancroft comes to the edge of the 'ice' and kneels on the steps, near her, D'Arcy to his R. Martin holds Kitty back

Kitty (*screaming*) Her hand! Look at her hand!

Kitty turns her face into Martin, as Frau Gessler, moaning, holds up the bloody rags

Steiner She's lost her hand.
Bancroft It's been cut!—quite cleanly!—straight through the bone!
Otto (*to Frau Gessler*) Was ist mit dir passiert?
Frau Gessler Da war eine Wolfsfalle—gestern Abend—ich habe das bewusst sein verloren—ich bin gerade wieder zu mir gekommen.
Otto She says it happened last night. Her hand was caught in a wolf-trap. She fainted and has only now recovered. (*Thoughtfully*) At least, that is what she *says*.
D'Arcy Fairly common sort of accident around here, what? I take it that's how you lost your own hand.
Otto (*fighting the hand still*) No.
Steiner Whatever happened, she needs immediate treatment. Bring her to my laboratory.
Frau Gessler (*terrified*) Nein! Nein! (*She pulls away from him towards Bancroft*)
Steiner Don't be foolish, Frau Gessler. I can help you. Ich kann Ihnen helfen.
Frau Gessler Nein! Nein! Sie nicht! Sie nicht!
Otto She doesn't seem to care for your methods, Professor.
Steiner She's hysterical. Drag her.

Steiner grabs her handless wrist and begins to drag her off. The furious Bancroft jumps to his feet

Bancroft No!

Steiner pauses, looking at him

Whatever the reason, she's frightened. (*He kicks off his overshoes and bends over Frau Gessler*) Do you mind if *I* treat you?
Otto Der Englische Arzt fragt dich, ober helfen darf.
Frau Gessler (*gratefully*) Ja, bitte, Herr Doktor. Vielen dank. Vielen dank.
Bancroft Bring her, D'Arcy.

D'Arcy skates to the step, kicks off his overshoes, goes to Frau Gessler, and helps Bancroft with her

(*to Mrs Bancroft*) I'll see you later, my dear.

They help Frau Gessler out. As soon as they have gone, Martin angrily removes his overshoes and flings them down with the others, remaining on the 'ice' and glaring at Otto

Martin (*furious*) Und jetzt, Herr Inspektor, möchten Sie uns das vielleicht erklären!

Steiner Please, Martin, we have guests. In English, if you don't mind. (*He gently picks up the table and chair and sets them out of the way DL*)

Martin (*crossing to the step and glaring up at Otto*) I am asking this officious pig who dared to set such a trap in my forest!

Otto I'm afraid I don't know, Baron.

Martin You lie! (*He climbs the step to glare at Otto*)

Steiner, watching amusedly, sits on the table. Kitty holds on to Mrs Bancroft's arm, listening

Otto Not even *you* can prove that.

Martin I have forbidden such traps to be set! Only one person would dare disobey me! You, Otto! You, with your pathological hatred of wolves!

Mrs Bancroft But surely, Baron, doesn't *everybody* dislike wolves?

Martin Only cretins and superstitious simpletons . . . Such as Otto became when he lost his hand.

Otto's hand twitches and jumps. Otto controls it

Do you know what a wolf is? Does anybody know?

Mrs Bancroft (*vaguely*) I think I saw one in Regent's Park once. Or was it a bear? It was one of those animals.

Martin But you all have a picture of the wolf in your minds, do you not? . . . A vision? . . . Oh yes, I see it clearly . . .

Minor music underlays

A cunning, perfidious creature, is it not? . . . Red-eyed and cruel . . . devouring alive little children and old grandmothers? . . .

Otto It has been known.

Martin Only when the animal is desperate . . . Hungry and frightened and hunted . . .

The music becomes gentler. During the following, D'Arcy comes on quietly from DL, crossing Steiner to R, listening

Consider this creature for a moment. He is a beautiful, adapted, social animal. (*He crosses slowly, in front of Mrs Bancroft and Kitty*) He lives in the eternal snows, like a child, in a civilised family—a group with a structure as decent and as gentle as any human organism. He hunts and kills, yes, but only for food—only to live. And he mates for life . . . unlike *some* animals.

The music ends

Mrs Bancroft Please, Baron, there are some subjects best avoided.
D'Arcy Even in wolves.

They turn and look at him. Mrs Bancroft moves L to the step

Mrs Bancroft Oh, there you are, D'Arcy. Is everything all right?
D'Arcy Yes, the Doctor's treating her now.

Mrs Bancroft sits on the step and takes off her overshoes, during the following, handing them to D'Arcy, who also collects up the others

Steiner (*faintly amused by it all*) You must forgive Martin's little outburst, my dear. You see, he loves wolves. In fact, he is a great authority. He has written many books.
Kitty I think it's wonderful.
Martin Well, I can't prevent their being hunted, but I can and do prevent traps being set and poison being laid.
Otto Even when the traps are not set only for the wolf himself?

Minor chords

Mrs Bancroft What do you mean, Inspector?
Otto I mean there are not only wolves in the forest.
Mrs Bancroft What else?
Otto You will have to ask Frau Gessler when she has recovered. But this much I *do* know—her hand was not caught in any trap. It had been cut—cleanly—with a knife.

A brief pause, then Ernst appears at the rear of the auditorium—a cheerful, drunken hunter, dressed in a warm jacket, carrying a rifle and a game-bag over his shoulder

Ernst Guten Tag! Eine schöne Nacht, was? Habt ihr euch gut unterhalten? Ja, das dacht ich mir! Ich auch!
Martin (*looking out at him in disgust*) Der Schweinhund!
Kitty Who is it?
Martin A drunken oaf—one of those damned hunters I can do nothing about. He has been shooting wolves for the bounty.
Otto Perhaps he saw something of Frau Gessler's accident. (*Calling out to Ernst*) Haben Sie Frau Gessler gesehen?
Ernst (*coming slowly down the aisle*) Nein. Niemanden. Nur einen grossen Wolf. Den habe ich geschossen.
Otto Kommen Sie her!

Ernst makes his way to the steps up to stage

Mrs Bancroft What did he say?
Otto He says, "No, he didn't see her". All he saw all night was one big wolf. He shot it. He has the pad in his bag.
Kitty The pad?
Martin Yes, it is the law. In order to get his bounty—his blood money— he must produce a wolf's pad—one of its paws.
Ernst (*as he climbs the steps*) Sie ist schön und gross. Ich zeige sie Ihnen.
Otto He wants to show it to us.

Quiet, minor music, building to a crescendo during the following. Kitty recoils against Martin as Ernst comes to the centre

Kitty Oh no, if he doesn't mind, I'd really rather not.
Otto Oh, but he insists. He is very proud of it. It is one of the biggest wolves he has ever killed.
Martin Look at it, my dear. Look at it and see how we mutilate God's creatures—how this drunken cretin earns his money . . . Look at it!

During this, the grinning Ernst has been fumbling in his bag. He now produces a woman's hand. At the sight of it, he shrieks, drops it, and backs away. Otto comes forward and kneels beside it. Martin crosses in front of Kitty. D'Arcy crouches on the step, behind Otto. Steiner rises

Otto A woman's hand!
D'Arcy How can you tell?
Otto There is nail varnish?
D'Arcy That doesn't always follow.
Otto The wedding ring is still on the finger. (*He twists and looks up to Ernst, who is mumbling and crossing himself*) Kommen Sie zurück!

Ernst stumbles up the step onto the rostrum

Kommen Sie sofort zurück!

Otto rises, but Ernst, with a cry, has run off

(*Meaningfully*) So! . . . There are only wolves in the forest? . . .

Faint wolf-howl. The light is fast fading. The pale moon shows—rather suddenly. Eerie, tinkling music. Faint sound of wind

Mrs Bancroft The moon's coming out.
Otto Yes. (*Suddenly*) Your husband! We must go to him immediately! He may be in great danger!
Mrs Bancroft What? Why?
Otto There's no time to explain! We must hurry! Follow me!

Otto hurries out

Mrs Bancroft (*following him*) Come along, D'Arcy!
D'Arcy (*loathe to leave Kitty with Martin*) I'm coming, Mrs Bancroft. I'm *always* coming!

D'Arcy follows her off DL. Kitty half goes to follow them, but Martin restrains her gently. Steiner moves R a little, smiling at them silkily, then turns and goes. The light fades. The moon grows brighter. The music turns romantic. Martin cups Kitty's face in his hands

Martin This is how I will always remember you—lit by moonlight.

He bends to kiss her. Lights fade to BLACKOUT, *the moon last. Music to climax, then fade to throbbing, minor chords*

B

SCENE 5

A Room in the Castle

The music continues gently, ominously, as dim light gathers high up on the rostrum DR. Frau Gessler sits in a small wooden chair, L. Bancroft kneels beside her, his doctor's bag open on the floor beside him, and is just completing bandaging her wrist. Loose bandages are scattered on the floor. The UR arch has been covered by two louvred shutters, and the UL arch by a gauze or a black leg. A red special spot picks out the edge of the rostrum in front of the chair, indicating a fire. Frau Gessler's eyes gleam as she watches him carefully, seductively

Bancroft There, that should do it. But we must get you to a hospital as soon as possible.

Frau Gessler The nearest hospital is 80 kilometres away.

Bancroft Then we must make arrangements as soon as you're fit to travel. That's a very serious wound.

Frau Gessler Not really—I'm left-handed.

Bancroft, who is putting gear away into his bag, suddenly pauses

Bancroft I say, I've just noticed! You're speaking remarkably good English.

Frau Gessler Yes. I learn languages from the Professor.

Bancroft Steiner? Why should he teach you?

Frau Gessler I work as a nurse for him once . . . and some of the patients are coming from England.

Bancroft Like that poor chap, Ramsey, for example? (*He crosses to R and puts his bag outside, through the archway*)

Frau Gessler Ramsey? . . . Oh yes. Although his condition is not so serious, or so—developed—as others.

Bancroft (*turning to her*) Developed? You make it sound as though Konrad makes his patients worse.

Frau Gessler I do? (*Laughing a little*) Silly of me.

Bancroft (*going to her*) You look a little faint. Shall I get you a drink?

Frau Gessler That is not necessary, thank you.

Bancroft A brandy. Now that will do you good.

Frau Gessler I never drink—alcohol.

Bancroft Water, then.

Frau Gessler I never drink—water.

Bancroft No alcohol, no water? What else is there?

Frau Gessler Oh . . . (*She teases at the edge of her bandages with her teeth, her eyes mocking him. Minor music underlays*)

Bancroft Now that's curious.

Frau Gessler What is?

Bancroft Your eyes—they seem to be reflecting the light from the fire. (*He indicates front of rostrum*)

Frau Gessler Don't everybody's?

Bancroft Not the human eye. Nocturnal animals have a reflecting pigment which shines in the dark, but . . . It's obviously an optical illusion.

Frau Gessler (*facing away from him, front*) Exactly that, Doctor.
Bancroft Yes, right, well . . . (*He crosses behind her and picks up the bandages*) I'd better clear away these bandages. (*He goes down the steps to exit*)
Frau Gessler (*rising*) No! Don't go! Please!

Bancroft pauses, turning to look at her

I'm still a little weak. I'd rather you stayed with me.
Bancroft (*uneasy—not sure why*) Well, it *is* getting rather late.

Frau Gessler turns and moves up to the louvred shutters, spreading her hands out on them

Frau Gessler Yes, the moon will be out. We shall see her through the trees.
Bancroft Yes, that's exactly what I mean.
Frau Gessler We can watch her grow bright together . . . She is a great friend when you live in the forest. (*Her hand slides to the handle that controls the louvres*)
Bancroft Quite.
Frau Gessler A companion . . . an ally . . . (*She suddenly depresses the handle, and the sky and the moon shine brightly through the slats. N.B. The louvres are, of course, not practical. It is a lighting cue behind them. The handle is a dummy. At the sight of the moon, Frau Gessler cries out and doubles up, as if in pain. Bancroft hurries back up the steps*)
Bancroft Are you in pain?
Frau Gessler No . . . no . . . it will pass. (*She makes a sudden little snarl. N.B. To heighten effect, all snarls and growls can be doubled off through a microphone*) Excuse me. (*She breathes heavily, loudly*)
Bancroft You don't look at all well, you know. Shock. That must be it. Delayed shock. I'd better get you a sedative. (*He turns*)
Frau Gessler No!
Bancroft (*turning to her*) But—
Frau Gessler I'm all right, I tell you! I don't need that! (*She growls deep in her throat, her nails tearing at the louvres, making a horrid noise*)
Bancroft (*not knowing where to put himself*) Shock . . . Yes . . . That must be it.

Gasping, Frau Gessler tries to control herself, leaning back against the louvres

Frau Gessler Why don't you join me, Doctor?
Bancroft Over there?
Frau Gessler Yes . . . Be *near* me . . . Your patient . . . Don't you want that?
Bancroft Certainly . . . If it'll make you feel better. (*He goes to climb the steps, pausing, as a sudden deep rumble comes from her throat*) What's that noise?
Frau Gessler I'm sorry—a touch of bronchitis. Don't be alarmed. (*She snarls suddenly, then controls it. She holds out her arms, her voice now calm, seductive, hypnotic. Treble trills on the piano*) Come to me, Doctor.

You can't refuse. Come to me.

Bancroft I . . .

Frau Gessler Come, Doctor, come . . . Tend my fever . . . Nurse my pain . . . Come . . . Come . . .

Hypnotised, Bancroft drops the bandages, climbs the steps. The moon seems to grow brighter. The rumbling in her throat turns to a deep purring. Her teeth are bared. Her nails reach out for his neck. As they do so . . . Otto rushes in UR

Otto Zur Seite!

He works the 'handle' at the louvred windows, and the moon vanishes. The music stops, the spell broken. Frau Gessler collapses with a sigh that turns into short hysterics. Bancroft shakes his head, breaking away. D'Arcy and Mrs Bancroft hurry in from UR, followed a little later by Steiner who stands in the entrance, watching. D'Arcy looks strangely at Frau Gessler, then crosses behind her and goes down the steps to Bancroft

D'Arcy Are you all right, Sir?

Bancroft What? . . . I don't know. (*He shakes his head, then calls across to Steiner*) Konrad, what the devil's going on here? She says she's a nurse of yours, but if you ask me she ought to be a bloody patient!

Mrs Bancroft Language, Hugo.

Bancroft Beg pardon, my dear.

Steiner What happened?

Bancroft I'm not sure. I don't seem to recall too clearly. But she was certainly behaving in the strangest way.

Otto I think *I* can explain.

During this, Frau Gessler has crawled forward to the edge of the rostrum. Minor chords as Otto moves to her

Frau Gessler, I have a very serious question to put to you, and I demand the truth. (*He takes the hand from his pocket and holds it out to her*) Do you identify this hand?

Frau Gessler (*examining it*) Yes, it's mine.

Otto How can you be sure?

Frau Gessler I recognise the mole.

Otto Mole? What are you talking about, mole? There are no moles here —they hibernate during the winter.

Frau Gessler Can I have it back, please?

Otto No. It is evidence. (*He puts it back in his pocket*)

Frau Gessler Evidence? Of what? I told you where I lost it—in a trap.

Otto But that is not where we found it, Frau Gessler. Ernst the Hunter says he cut it from a wolf.

Minor chords

Frau Gessler Ernst is a drunken fool. He would say anything.

Steiner She is right, Inspector. Clearly, Ernst found the hand in his trap, and the rest is pure imagination.

Bancroft In other words, *he*'s crackers as well. I don't know why you don't lock up the whole damn village.
Otto There is another explanation.

Minor chords

(*To Steiner*) I think you know what I mean.

Minor chords

Steiner (*contemptuously*) I won't even hear of it. It's superstitious absurdity.
Mrs Bancroft Hear *what*? Kindly explain yourself, Professor. My head is spinning.
Steiner Very well, since you insist, Mrs Bancroft. The Inspector is suggesting that Frau Gessler is suffering from a rather rare form of lycanthropy—

Minor chords

In fact, the real thing.

Minor chords

Bancroft You mean—?
Steiner Yes. He thinks she's a werewolf.

Minor chords resolve

Bancroft But that's ridiculous.
Steiner For once, Bancroft, our diagnoses agree.
Mrs Bancroft Surely you can't believe in such things, Inspector?
Otto I believe that the circumstances require further investigation, and that in the meantime Frau Gessler should accompany me to the cells— for her own protection.
Bancroft Protection? From what?
Steiner From the other villagers, I'm afraid to say. They sometimes take it into their heads to burn suspected werewolves.
Bancroft (*incredulously*) In *1922*?
Steiner Especially in 1922.
Otto (*to Frau Gessler*) Wenn Sie mir bitte folgen möchten, Frau Gessler.

She rises. Otto indicates the door UR. Steiner moves to allow her room to pass through. She pauses before him, laughs sharply, spits in his face and goes off. Otto regards him a moment, then follows her off. Steiner moves a little, wiping his face with a handkerchief

Steiner Die Hündin!
Bancroft (*climbing steps to Mrs Bancroft*) That's one young lady you don't seem to go down too well with, Konrad.
Steiner Geniuses are always misunderstood.
Bancroft I wouldn't know. I've never met one. (*To Mrs Bancroft*) Eunice. (*He indicates entrance UR, and follows her out*)

D'Arcy climbs steps, goes to the entrance, pauses, looks back at Steiner, goes

Steiner (*to himself*) Frau Gessler ... (*He turns suddenly and goes out. Fade to* BLACKOUT. *Minor music*)

SCENE 6

The Cells

During the BLACKOUT, *the small arch UC, in which the small wooden door is still folded back out of sight, is filled with a cell-door, apparently made of iron bars. The Police Sergeant, tunic unbuttoned, sits on the bench R of this poor, reading a newspaper. Otto appears through the bars*

Otto Achtung!

The Sergeant drops the paper, jumps to his feet and hastily buttons his tunic. Otto opens the barred door and pushes Frau Gessler in

Otto Setzen Sie sich. Dorthin.
Frau Gessler Stossen Sie mich nicht so, Sie schwein!
Otto Tun Sie, was ich Ihnen sage.

Steiner appears behind them

Steiner (*indicating Frau Gessler*) Ich möchte ein paar Worte mit der Gefangen sprechen.
Otto (*shaking his head*) Das ist nicht erlaubt.
Steiner Ich will trotzdem mit ihr reden.
Otto (*giving in*) Also gut. (*To the Sergeant*) Verlassen Sie den Raum nicht.
Sergeant Zu Befehl.

Otto goes out through the barred door.

Steiner smiles at the Sergeant who stands self-consciously on guard by the door, as he speaks to Frau Gessler

Steiner Speak English in front of this fool.
Frau Gessler It will be my pleasure, Professor. I wondered how long it would take for you to arrive.
Steiner Really?
Frau Gessler You know what to do, Professor. These ignorant peasants will tear me limb from limb as soon as Ernst is sober enough to tell his story. By then, I must be gone out of here.
Steiner That will be difficult.
Frau Gessler Not for *you*, Professor. Not for *you*. Otherwise, I might weaken. I might feel the need to tell what I know in exchange for my liberty.
Steiner I see.

Minor chords

Frau Gessler You will do something, Professor? You will—*do* something?
Steiner Oh, we'll do something for you. Don't worry about that.

Otto returns, through the barred door, coat off, braces showing, carrying papers

Auf wiederseh'n, meine liebe.

Frau Gessler Auf wiederseh'n.

Steiner looks at Otto and exits UC

Otto thoughtfully looks off after him, at the Sergeant, and then speaks to Frau Gessler in English

Otto It will be better for you if you tell the truth.

Frau Gessler (*mockingly*) How did you lose your hand, Otto?

The hand convulses as he stiffens. She laughs malignantly

Wie hast du deine Hand verloren, Otto?

Otto (*In fury, he smashes his hand against his thigh to quieten it, then shouts at the Sergeant*) Du! Komm mit mir!

Sergeant Jawohl, Herr Inspektor!

They exit UC, the Sergeant making great play of locking the door behind him, and bolting it. Left alone, Frau Gessler looks at her hands, goes to the bars of the door, feels their strength

Frau Gessler (*to herself*) Zu müde . . . Zu müde . . .

She goes to the bench and stretches out on it, preparing for sleep. Light slowly fades to a dim pool of blue light on her. The piano plays a sombre little bridge—a passage of time. A soft grunting is heard, and a blue special inside the rostrum glows softly, lighting the bars of the door from behind. A dark shapeless mass appears beyond the door, breathing heavily. It is important that during this scene we can make out no details of the figure—no face, or mask. All growls and snarls in this scene should be doubled off-stage through a microphone. Frau Gessler wakes up

Wer ist da? . . . (*She sees the figure—at first with relief*) Oh, du bist es. Du bist gekommen um mich zu holen—endlich.

The figure lets out a long, low growl. Her pleasure changes to terror

Nein! Nein! Was machst du? . . . Hilfe! Hilfe!

The figure takes hold of the bars and with terrible strength slowly bends them apart. It is important that the bars are well lit, although the figure is not, that they are good and thick, and that the figure bends them apart very slowly. A twanging of metal, and then music from the piano. Frau Gessler shrieks and cowers. With a bound, the figure is into the cell and onto her. She gives a terrible scream. A loud growling and wet slobbering, then her body hits the floor, and the figure puts a foot on it, lifting up its head and letting out a long wolf-howl

Otto (*off*) Was ist los?

With an animal-like leap, the creature leaps up onto the high rostrum and disappears. Otto rushes through the mangled door, followed by the Sergeant. A little more light fades up as they peer at Frau Gessler

Mein Gott!

The Sergeant feels sick, but Otto pulls himself together

Holt alle Leute! Es gibt ein Ungeheuer im Dorf!

The Sergeant takes out a whistle and blows it, turning to go, and almost colliding with Steiner as he runs in past the mangled door. The Sergeant runs out

Steiner Was ist los?

Otto indicates the body. Steiner looks down at her, then starts and appears to pick up something from the floor. He shows it to Otto. It is the penny whistle

Otto Ramsey!
Steiner Jawohl! . . . Schnell! Wir müssen ihn finden!

The Sergeant runs in, carrying two rifles and great-coats. He throws one of each to Otto, and both run off out again, leaving Steiner alone. The sounds die behind them, as Steiner smiles cruelly

Ramsey . . .

Crashing finale music, and fade to BLACKOUT

SCENE 7

The Forest

The music segues in the BLACKOUT *to a gentle tinkle. Sounds of twittering birds. Golden sunlight, shaded with green, lights all the levels except the stage level in which the cell has just been played. The mangled door has been struck, and flown in front of the upstage arches is a gauze cloth depicting a forest scene. The trees on it are gnarled and twisted. About halfway downstage, a second header is flown in, with a graceful cut-piece extending down towards the rostrum area, L. Almost childish laughter heard off, UR, from Martin and Kitty*

Kitty (*off*) No, Martin, no!

She runs on, and off again through the arch UR. Martin runs on, looking for her. He, too, runs off through the arch. Kitty reappears through the arch UL, and runs down the stairs, and hides, partially concealed, in the DL entrance. Martin reappears through the arch

Martin Kitty? . . . Where are you? . . . Here Kitty, here Kitty! . . . (*He comes forward to the steps and sees her*) I see you . . . I see you. (*He comes slowly down the steps. Giggling, Kitty runs on from her hiding place and turns front, about to run directly into the audience and over the DL trap. Martin's good-humour immediately changes to alarm*) Stop! For God's sake, stop! (*He runs to her and pulls her back*)
Kitty What is it? What's wrong? (*Martin indicates the trap*)
Martin You see how green it is there. We're on the edge of the swamp.

It is a bog. Many an unwary traveller has been lost in there. We're safe
here.

They sit on the edge of the rostrum

Kitty It's beautiful, the forest—but rather menacing as well.
Martin I love it. And yet—(*he pauses*)
Kitty Yet?
Martin Sometimes I find it so lonely. I'm always on my own, you see.
Kitty Surely you've got *some* friends. What about Professor Steiner?
Martin Well, yes, there is Konrad. But that's not the sort of friendship
I'm talking about.

A brief pause. They listen to the birdsong

Your father and he were very close once, were they not?
Kitty Yes, they were students together. But there was some trouble. I
never found out what. The Professor had to leave.
Martin He's a great man. He does wonderful work.
Kitty And yet he buries himself away here. I wonder why that is.
Martin Nobody knows. He just arrived one day and offered to rent part
of my castle. Such an amount! I couldn't refuse.

Faint distant shouts and whistles are heard

Kitty What's that?
Martin It must be Otto and his search-party—looking for that poor
maniac Ramsey.
Kitty Yes. (*Shivering*) The bars of that woman's cell were bent like . . .
Insanity must give one amazing strength.
Martin Don't be afraid. He won't sneak up on us. I've got very acute
hearing.
Kitty Oh, I know I'm safe with you. But all the same, I'm glad Mummy
doesn't know where we are. She'd only forbid it. So would D'Arcy if he
dared.
Martin D'Arcy? Your butler?
Kitty Yes.

Martin rises and moves a little L

Martin Forgive me saying so, Kitty, but that man behaves above his
station.
Kitty I know. He's rather sweet.
Martin Sometimes, he makes me feel so—so—
Kitty What?
Martin Jealous.
Kitty D'Arcy? . . . I'll tell him. Perhaps it will make him feel better.

*Romantic music underlays. The twittering birds fade. Martin takes her hands,
and lifts her to her feet*

Martin Oh Kitty, if only you could stay with me!
Kitty And if I could?

Martin We should walk the forest together, you and I, hand in hand, stars
in our eyes, and we should sit together on the green moss . . .

Kitty And then?

Martin And then we should be together . . . Isn't that enough?

*During the song, the lighting becomes very romantic. Little white rabbits in
pairs (glove puppets) pop up and watch, dancing and embracing with them*

SONG: **This Is The Start**

Martin	All my life I've waited Patiently for this I thought that I was fated Always bound to miss Now at last it's happened And I know it's happened It's really happened now
	This is the start A new beginning It's just beginning For me and for you
Both	No more apart We'll be together So close together For ever with you
Martin **Kitty**	It's clear to see this was meant to be Ah ha ha . . . .
Martin **Kitty**	You are the key to eternity Ah ha ha . . . .
Kitty	This is the start Of our new romance Yes, our new romance It never will die
Both	So take my heart It's yours completely I say completely
Kitty	I don't have to lie
Martin	She doesn't have to lie
Both	(*harmony*) It's clear to see this would always be Oh don't you see, it's our destiny

*They do a little foxtrot dance, very simple and formal, to one orchestral verse
and middle eight*

This is the start
Our new beginning
It's just beginning
For me and for you

They embrace. As they do so, a body falls from behind the gauze, to their left. Crashing minor chords. Lights dim. Kitty screams. Martin comforts her, then moves her a little R before kneeling to examine the body

Martin It's Ernst, the hunter.

Minor chords

Kitty He's—he's—
Martin Yes, I know. Don't look.
Kitty But his head—his head! Who could have done such a thing?
Martin It's typical of a wolf attack.

Minor chords

Kitty What is?
Martin They bite at the head first—until it is severed.
Kitty (*shuddering, putting face in her hands*) Oh, don't!
Martin He must have been very careless—or drunk—and a pack pulled him down. Except—
Kitty Except what?
Martin I'm sure there isn't a pack in the forest at the moment. Besides, he was a *hunter*—he would have his gun.

He searches near the body, gives a sudden exclamation, and lifts up Ernst's gun. The barrel is bent almost double. Minor chords. Faint shouts and whistles

Listen. I must go and fetch Otto. You stay here.
Kitty Oh no, I couldn't.
Martin He's only just over the rise. It won't take a moment. Have courage, Kitty (*He kisses her quickly*) I love you.

He runs up the steps, and out UR

Kitty But Martin ... ! Martin ... !

Pause

He's gone.

Tinkling, menacing music. The lights dim further. A cold wind blows

The sun's going in ... Oh, the days are so *short* around here!

Pause. She calls out
Martin! Hurry up!

Music a little louder. The moon begins to glow through the gauze as lights fade further and the wind rises

Oh, Mother! ...

Louder wind in a sudden gust. A soft rustling of trees

What's that?

The gauze begins to twitch and tremble, as if somebody were behind it

What's that?

She begins to back away, downstage

There's somebody in there! Who is it?

The gauze sways and rustles alarmingly

Martin!

She takes a final step backwards onto the trap, and immediately sinks down to her waist in the 'bog'. Bubbling, sucking sound. She screams and begins to sink further. She claws at the ground, and seems to have safely supported herself when the gauze twitches aside and a hideous, hairy face peers out at her. A long arm ending in a furry, clawed paw, reaches out for her. She screams and sinks back down into the 'bog'

D'Arcy (*off*) Over here! It came from over here!
Kitty (*screaming*) D'Arcy!

D'Arcy rushes on, carrying a rifle. He stares down at the scene

D'Arcy Good God!

He aims at the face and fires, the rifle making a tremendous bang. The gauze dances violently as the figure vanishes through the DL entrance

Kitty D'Arcy!

D'Arcy Coming, Miss Bancroft! Coming!

He runs down the two levels to her, throws himself flat, and holds out a hand to her

It's all right, Miss Bancroft. I've got you.

He manages to reach her hand, but it is a terrible struggle dragging her clear, and he dare go no closer himself. Otto rushes on UR, also armed

Otto What is it? What did you shoot?
D'Arcy A wolf, I think.
Otto What do you mean, you only think? Don't you know a wolf when you see one?
D'Arcy No! They're not very common in Kensington! And give me a hand here! This mud is damn tenacious!

Otto runs down and holds on to D'Arcy's legs while he slowly pulls Kitty clear. Music change to major

Martin (*off*) Kitty! Kitty!
Kitty Over here, Martin!

D'Arcy pulls her free. Otto prowls, examining gauze and entrance. Martin runs on and hurries down to her, kneeling beside her, pushing D'Arcy aside, who rises

Martin Oh Kitty, how can you ever forgive me?

Kitty It's all right, Martin, I'm safe now *you're* here.
D'Arcy (*sarcastically*) Oh yes, it's a good job *you* turned up.
Martin I'm so sorry.
D'Arcy I should damn well think you are. How dare you leave Miss
   Bancroft alone at a time like this? Any *other* time, of course . . .
Kitty Please, D'Arcy, don't scold him. I know he meant well.
D'Arcy So did the Kaiser.

Otto turns in the entrance and glares at him

Martin You're quite right to be angry. But thank you for your assistance.
D'Arcy Not at all.
Otto (*indicating gauze*) I think you winged him.
Martin Him?
Otto It. There is blood here.

   Steiner hurries on

Steiner What happened? Have you found Ramsey?
Kitty No, but we certainly found *something*.
Martin Over here in the bushes, Konrad.
Steiner It's Ernst. Poor devil. It must have been a wolf.
D'Arcy There's blood on your hand, Professor. How did that happen?
Steiner Oh, I must have caught it on a bramble. It's nothing serious.

*Otto reaches across with his dead hand and takes hold of Steiner's hand,
looking at it suspiciously*

Otto This will all need to be fully investigated. I shall need to interrogate
   everybody immediately.
Steiner I hardly think there can be any point in doing that until we have
   found Ramsey, Inspector.
Otto You think Ramsey did this?
Steiner Don't you?
Otto Just now you said it was a wolf.
Steiner Well, perhaps it is not so different. You know his malady.
Otto I know what I am told about it. Please, Baron, take Miss Bancroft
   to the castle. You go there too, Professor. D'Arcy and I will join you
   later.

Pause. Nobody moves

   Does something detain you, Professor?
Steiner You're holding my hand.

Otto prises it apart

Martin Come, Kitty.

   He leads her up the steps and off. Steiner follows them

D'Arcy There's something fishy going on here.
Otto You feel that, do you?

D'Arcy Yes. I don't believe that chap Ramsey did all this. He was such a harmless-looking little coot.

Otto Then you think it was a wolf?

D'Arcy I don't know.

Otto Well, we shall see. And listen—no more snide remarks about the Kaiser, all right? . . . Give me a hand to put this body somewhere safe. I'll take his legs and you take his head—it's over there somewhere.

They begin to drag the body off

And hurry up! I don't want to be caught out here too long at night.

Music. Fade to BLACKOUT

SCENE 8

Walpurgisdorf Castle

During the BLACKOUT, *fly out gauzes and reset the chair as in Scene 2. Either side of the small arch UC are set two tall candelabra, with practical candles in them, and the small, studded, wooden door has been reset in this entrance. A dim moon is seen through the UL entrance. Bancroft and Mrs Bancroft come on DR, dressed in evening clothes, as Ingeborg comes out of the UC arch, carrying a tray with drinks on it. She crosses up the steps L*

Bancroft Ah Ingeborg, there you are. Tell me—is dinner ready yet?

Ingeborg Nein (*She begins to arrange bottles and glasses on the table above the DL entrance*)

Mrs Bancroft We were told it was eight.

Ingeborg Ja.

Mrs Bancroft Well, isn't it eight now?

Ingeborg Nein.

Mrs Bancroft What's the silly Frau talking about?

Bancroft I think perhaps you had better let me handle this, my dear. (*He crosses L to the steps*) Now tell me, Ingeborg, have the others returned from the search-party yet?

Ingeborg turns to look at him looking puzzled. He tries it in pidgin German

Ist alles rückwarts von der suchen partei jetzt?

Ingeborg (*speaking very rapidly*) Nein, aber man erwartet Sie jeden Augenblick. Warum können Sie nicht Ihre Klappe halten und ruhig auf Sie warten. Ich habe keine Zeit für unnützes Geschwätz.

Bancroft (*who hasn't a clue what she's talking about*) Ah good, that's settled that. Meanwhile, we'd like some drinks, please. A lightly chilled Tio Pepe for myself, and a sweet martini with a dash of grenadine and a slice of lemon for my dear lady wife.

Ingeborg We got brandy and we got beer. Which do you want?

Bancroft Well . . . Good heavens, you speak English!

Ingeborg Ja, deedly, I speak it wellington. I come back with the beer.

Bancroft But we don't *want* beer!
Ingeborg OK, I don't come back at all.

She goes out. Bancroft turns to find Mrs Bancroft glaring at him

Mrs Bancroft (*scornfully*) Old school chum! . . . Trees! . . . Walpurgisdorf!
. . . Werewolves!
Bancroft Well, at least we can settle down to a nice meal, when it comes. I
must admit it's been a somewhat nerve-wracking visit so far, so I tell you
what . . . You just put your feet up and relax by the fire.

He helps her to sit and then sits on the arm beside her

There we are, my dear. Quite comfy?

*She rests her head happily against his shoulder. As she does so, there is a
bang off, a sudden loud gust of wind, and Steiner, Kitty, Martin, D'Arcy
and Otto come on DL to a swirl of snowflakes, shedding their topgear,
and all immediately making for the fire in front of the Bancroft's chair.
Mrs Bancroft rises and backs away as they do so*

Steiner Ingeborg!

She immediately appears

Bring some brandy. It's been a long cold day.

*He throws his coat carelessly on the chair—enveloping Bancroft. Ingeborg
goes to the table and prepares brandies*

D'Arcy Can I get you a chair, Miss Bancroft?
Martin No, Kitty, sit over by the fire—it's warmer.
Kitty Thank you, Martin.

He leads her over to the bench below the entrance

Steiner And Ingeborg, when you've done that—ah! (*He jumps out of his
skin as the apparition of Bancroft, covered in the coat, rises. The coat falls
to the ground and Steiner recovers*) Bancroft, I didn't see you. Pick up
my coat, there's a good fellow.
D'Arcy (*coming round the chair to where Martin now kneels beside Kitty*)
Shall I fetch you a drink, Miss Bancroft?
Martin Ingeborg, a drink for Kitty. Immediately.

Steiner sits on the chair, warming his hands by the fire

Bancroft Did you find what you were looking for?
Steiner Rather more than we were looking for, I'm afraid. There's been
another murder.
Mrs Bancroft Good heavens! It's worse than Whitechapel!
Bancroft Committed by the same person?
Otto (*who has lingered L and is glaring at the occupants of the room*) Well—
let us just say that Mr Ramsey is still missing.
D'Arcy Shall I fetch your shawl, Miss Bancroft?

Martin Here, Kitty—use my coat. It's more comfortable. (*He drapes his coat over her shoulders*)
Bancroft What's that grinding noise?
Mrs Bancroft (*to D'Arcy*) D'Arcy! Stop gnashing your teeth! It's setting my nails on edge.

Fuming, D'Arcy retires and sits on the bench sulkily. Otto clears his throat

Otto Ladies and gentlemen, your attention, please. It is necessary that we discuss the situation in which we find ourselves.
Bancroft What is there to discuss? One of Konrad's patients is loose and out on the rampage. (*To Steiner*) I *did* warn you he was dangerous.
Otto And yet Mr Ramsey has been with us many months. Why has this violence not manifested itself earlier?
Steiner I daresay his condition got worse.
Otto But why should that be, Professor? Is he not here to be cured?
Steiner (*with grim good humour*) Oh no, I never *cure* my patients. I always take the greatest care never to do that.

Steiner takes a drink offered by Ingeborg who then offers one to Mrs Bancroft, Bancroft, Kitty, Martin and Otto in that order, during the following. Otto refuses

Mrs Bancroft Really? Why not?

Steiner rises and offers the seat to Mrs Bancroft during the following

Steiner Well, you see, the trouble is that a patient invents a delusional system—such as Ramsey's belief that he is a wolf—in order to protect himself against deeper and more dangerous disturbances...
Mrs Bancroft So if you cure him—?
Steiner He *really* gets ill. That's the trouble with orthodox psychoanalysis. Eventually, it becomes the very disease of which the patient is seeking a cure.
Bancroft Poppycock, Konrad. This is the kind of nonsense that got you thrown out of Medical School. That and— (*He pauses*)
Otto Yes, Professor? And—?
Bancroft *And* experimenting on mental patients without permission.
Steiner And whose permission should I have asked?
Bancroft Why, good heavens, some normal person's who was responsible for them!
Steiner But there is no such thing.

Minor chords. Music underlays all the following

Mrs Bancroft Nobody responsible for them? I can't believe it.
Steiner I mean, there is nobody *normal*.

Stronger chords in the underlay

This is my great discovery! *Nobody is normal!* ... Nobody! ... Anywhere in the world!
Bancroft Rubbish.

Steiner (*rounding on him*) But my dear Bancroft, you are a perfect example of what I mean.

Bancroft (*astonished*) I?

Steiner Of course. Look at yourself. There you stand, a successful Doctor, a good husband and father, mildly irascible, hen-pecked and hounded by your family, sleepless with ambition, riddled with responsibility, confined forever within the rigid perimeters of your profession, forever unable to escape the dictates of a super-ego clamped upon you by your early environment. In fact, a nice normal person.

Mrs Bancroft (*indignantly*) I thought you just said there was no such thing?

Steiner My dear Mrs Bancroft, the subtle irony of my explanation seems somehow to have eluded you. (*Furiously*) I mean, of course, that your husband is a nice normal *sick* person! . . . a person with normal *phobias*, normal *complexes*, normal *frustrations*, normal *repressions*, normal *perversions*! . . . In a word—and to put it simply for *you*, Mrs Bancroft —normal *insanity*! . . . Your husband is nothing more nor less than a socially acceptable lunatic!

Heavier chords. He quietens a moment

But we are *all* normal in this way, Mrs Bancroft. All of us! Everybody in this room! . . .

Mrs Bancroft (*faintly*) I think I should like a Beecham's Powder.

Steiner It was Freud who first pointed the way—Freud, with his notion that all phobias spring from isolated traumatic incidents in childhood . . . But only *I* have taken this idea to its logical conclusion! Only *I* have understood that we must *all* go through these early traumatic experiences— all of us! . . . And why should we wish to avoid them? They are part of the ordinary process of growing-up . . . (*Ecstatically*) Ah, the happy onset of that first neurosis! Mental puberty! . . . Hairs growing on the libido . . . strange stirrings in the Id . . . And if you're *really* lucky, perhaps even a brush with one of the great *psychoses*! . . . Paranoia! . . . Schizophrenia! . . . Manic-depression! . . . in a word—*maturity*!

Loud wolf-howl outside. Minor chords. All start, except Steiner, who doesn't seem to hear it

No, ladies and gentlemen, nobody is normal! . . . Deep within us all is planted a tiny seed of insanity . . . And *I*—Konrad Steiner— the intellectual giant among the pygmies—can nurture this tiny seed into the sturdy growing plant of *insanity*!

By now, we are beginning to doubt his sanity. Quieter wolf-howl. The music begins to run down. Pause

Otto Yes. Well, now I will say what *I* think. Wolves do not account for what has happened here. Insanity does not account for what has happened here. There is only one thing left . . . the werewolf.

Minor chords

Bancroft Why not? If we're going to believe in Konrad, we might as well believe in werewolves, as well. Why not?

Otto Several facts have led me to this conclusion. Let me enumerate them for you.

Ramsey comes in quietly behind him from DL. He carries a bill-hook and the front of his shirt is drenched in blood. Otto does not see him, and the others are too frozen to say or do anything

Firstly, all the attacks have taken place on or around the full moon, the time when the werewolf finds it easiest to assume his wolf shape and go hunting man. Secondly, the face that D'Arcy saw in the swamp . . .

He becomes aware of their expressions, turns and sees Ramsey. He yells and recoils RC, tugging at his pistol futilely with his dead hand

Ramsey Excuse me, you didn't see a rabbit run this way, did you? He's led me a right merry dance, I can tell you.

Steiner (*quietly—to Ingeborg*) Stell dich hinter ihn.

Ingeborg (*quietly*) Zu Befehl. (*She begins to edge quietly behind Ramsey*)

Ramsey You couldn't miss him. He's grey, with long ears, four legs, a little white tail, and he's rather short of breath.

Steiner (*humouring him*) No, I don't think we have seen him, Ramsey. Why don't you come over here, and tell us about him?

Ramsey Well, I'd like to, but I really ought to get after him.

Steiner (*soothingly*) Now, Ramsey, there are plenty of other rabbits, Why, even now, Ingeborg has two very nice white ones in the kitchen—haven't you, Ingeborg?

Ingeborg (*behind Ramsey by now*) Jawohl, Herr Professor.

At the sound of her voice, Ramsey turns, bill-hook casual in his hand. She recoils. Ramsey turns back to the others, and Ingeborg resumes her stealthy approach behind him

Otto Mr Ramsey—might I enquire why there is so much blood on your shirt?

Ramsey Blood? What blood? Oh, *this* blood. I had a nose-bleed.

Otto Oh, I see.

Ramsey It was that blasted rabbit.

Otto He punched you on the nose.

Ramsey No, I was chasing him and I tripped over a root. Nearly got him too.

Swings the bill-hook, nearly decapitating Ingeborg behind him. She retreats, and then resumes her stealthy approach

Otto Like you got Frau Gessler in my cell?

Ramsey Frau Gessler?

Otto And Ernst, by the swamp?

Ramsey Oh, him.

Otto Yes.

Pause

Ramsey (*laughing slyly*) That wasn't me. It was the wolf.
Otto What wolf?
Ramsey It was the wolf. I saw him do it. The big wolf. (*He howls like a wolf*)
Steiner (*sharply*) Ingeborg, pack ihn!

Ingeborg gets Ramsey's throat in an arm-lock. The others start forward

It's all right. Ingeborg can handle him.

And, indeed, she can—easily. Steiner turns back into the room

You're quite right, Bancroft . . . Bancroft?

Bancroft's rather shame-faced head appears from behind the chair

You're quite right. He *was* dangerous. I made a mistake, I'm afraid.
Bancroft Funny sort of mistake.
Steiner (*to Ingeborg*) Take him below. Lock him up.
Otto One moment.

He moves towards Ramsey and takes the penny whistle out of his pocket

Mr Ramsey, do you identify this whistle as yours?
Ramsey Yes, but I wanted *her* to have it. (*He indicates Kitty*) Her! She's to have it! Give it to her!
D'Arcy Why?
Ramsey It's soothing. It's very soothing. (*To Kitty*) You try it. You'll like it. (*Shouting*) Give it to her!
Otto No. It is evidence.
Ramsey (*almost hysterical*) Give it to her! Give it to her!
Bancroft Better let her have it. You can always collect it back later.

Reluctantly, Otto crosses to the chair and hands it across to Kitty

Kitty Thank you, Mr Ramsey.
Steiner (*to Ingeborg*) Go on.
Ingeborg Sofort.

She drags Ramsey off through the small arch

Steiner Well, Inspector? Are you satisfied now?
Otto Yes. There seems no other explanation.
D'Arcy What did he mean by 'the wolf'?

Otto pauses

Steiner Clearly, he was talking about himself. Simple identification. Almost as good as a confession of guilt. I'll keep him locked up here for the night, and in the morning I'll send him to the State Asylum. Obviously he's too dangerous to be kept here.
Otto (*still troubled*) Yes . . . Yes, that much is obvious. Well, I will say goodnight. Auf Wiederseh'n.

Murmured goodnights. Otto goes. Steiner follows, looking off after Otto, well pleased

Steiner Poor Otto, he did so want it to be a werewolf. They're a passion
  with him. (*He turns to the others*) And now, ladies and gentlemen,
  shall we dine?
Mrs Bancroft After what I've just seen and heard? No, thank you. I
  shall retire for the night. Hugo! Kitty!

*She goes up the steps and crosses on to the high rostrum, waiting. Kitty
leaves Martin and follows her. Bancroft is still deep in thought. As Kitty
goes up the steps, Steiner moves towards her*

Steiner Oh Miss Bancroft, Otto has left the whistle behind. Perhaps you
  had better give it to me— for safe-keeping.
Kitty I'd rather not, if you don't mind.
Steiner I really must insist.
Kitty The poor man wanted *me* to have it. I shall keep it for the time
  being.
Steiner (*coldly*) Very well.

Kitty goes up the steps. Bancroft is ready to follow her

Bancroft And we, Konrad, shall leave first thing in the morning.

*Kitty stops, turns, looks at Martin. Martin moves below the chair. D'Arcy
looks between them*

  I'm sorry, but I really can't approve of what is going on here.
Kitty Oh, but Daddy—
Bancroft The subject is closed. Come, Kitty. (*He goes to her, takes her
  by her arm, takes her up the steps to where Mrs Bancroft waits, and all
  three go out, Kitty throwing one last despairing glance back at Martin,
  who watches her go*)
Steiner (*cheerfully*) Well, that's that settled. And now, if you'll excuse me,
  I'd best go and help Ingeborg with Ramsey. He may need a sedative.
  (*He goes off through the little arch*)
Martin You don't seem very satisfied, D'Arcy.
D'Arcy It's all too pat for me. But then, I'm only the butler. Just ignore me.
Martin Well, at least you won't have me as a rival for Kitty any more.
D'Arcy (*in pretended astonishment*) You? A rival? The thought never
  entered my head.
Martin Then we can shake hands. (*He holds out his hand. A pause*)
D'Arcy (*coldly*) You're too good to be true, Baron. (*He shakes the hand
  perfunctorily*) Goodnight. (*He runs quickly up the stairs and out after the
  others*)
Martin (*smiling to himself*) Too good to be true?

*Martin looks up at the moon. The room dims a little. The moon seems to
grow brighter. Martin coughs, making a gargling noise in his throat. He
turns front. He looks different—a wicked expression on his face. He laughs*

  Well, they caught their werewolf ... in a way. The *real* ones are
  much harder to find.

Musical introduction as he crosses to the table and pours another brandy

SONG: **They're Ever So Evil**

Martin   They don't like illumination
             They really look too ghastly in the light
             They sleep throughout the day
             In the nicest kind of way
             Then they wake up everybody in the night

He sings L, with brandy in his hand

             They live in the darkness
             They howl at the moon
             They don't like the sunlight
             Won't see them at noon
             They flourish in winter
             Uncommon in June
             They're ever so evil, awful, hateful
             And there's more . . .

             They're ever so nasty
             They're ever so vile
             But ever so friendly
             They kill with a smile
             They don't really hate you
             It's only their nature
             They're ever so evil, awful, hateful
             And there's more . . .

He dances a little as the song goes into major

             They're not very pretty
             They're not very clean
             They never go out much
             They never get seen
             But never despair now
             You'll know where they've been
             They're ever so evil, awful, hateful
             And there's more . . .

             They're secretive, werewolves
             They change in the dark
             One moment they're normal
             And then you remark
             They turn very frightful
             Won't stop at a biteful
             They're ever so evil, awful, hateful
             And there's more . . .
             They're ever so evil, awful, hateful
             And there's more . . .
             They're ever so evil, awful, hateful
             So much more.

At the end of the song, he roars with laughter. High-pitched music, and he folds forward, hugging his waist, as if in pain. He rolls on the floor. A loud wind begins to blow, becoming louder and louder throughout the following. He staggers to his feet and shakes fist at the moon

Not now, damn you! Not now! Not again!

He examines the backs of his hands in the moonlight, recoiling in horror at what he seems to see, then staggers over to the drinks table, and tries to pour a drink. The bottles crash to the floor, and he covers his face with his hands. We can now see hairy patches on the backs of his hands. He falls to the floor and rolls out of sight. He immediately rolls back in, hands still held to the face—but this time the hands are thick and hairy. He staggers across stage to the little arch UC and falls through, immediately reappearing. He pulls his hands away from his face. Tufts of hair are growing on the face. Again, he convulses, falls to the floor, rolls over and over, as if in agony. He staggers out DR, immediately reappearing. The face and hands are even hairier. He convulses, staggers, rolls his way to the entrance, UL, and falls through, immediately reappearing and falling DL. The face and hands are hairier. He falls out DL, immediately reappearing—this time, he has the full wolf-face and hands—the transformation is completed—and he leaps to C with a great bound, raises his head high and lets out a long howl. This is a production piece, managed by having at least two other actors of similar size and weight, dressed identically. The masks should go through definite transitions, continuous loud wind helps tension, growling and snarling throughout should be done through offstage microphones, all entrances should be immediate so that we can see there has been no time for an actual change offstage. And throughout, the bodily transformation should seem to cause great pain and discomfort. It should build in tension, pace and volume to the final entrance, at which the wind should be cut to a whisper, the long (offstage microphone) howl and subsequent snarling taking over. It will be very exciting if well-rehearsed and well-drilled. With a final shattering roar, Martin leaps into the auditorium, gibbering between the seats.

When some of the reaction has died down, Kitty creeps on from UR, shawl over her shoulders, and comes downstage

Kitty Martin? . . . I had to come to say goodbye . . . Martin? . . . Where are you?

Growling from the auditorium. She peers out at him

What are you doing out there?

Martin shambles down the aisle towards her. She backs off, terror-stricken, screaming. He leaps up onstage, hurling the chair aside. She faints. He picks her up, leaps back down into the aisle, rushes through the house and out. D'Arcy rushes on

D'Arcy Miss Bancroft? Did you call? . . . (*Seeing the room*) Good God! (*He jumps down and picks up Kitty's shawl*) Kitty . . . (*To the audience*) What happened to her?

With luck, somebody will tell him

It must have been Steiner! I never trusted that man!

With luck he will be contradicted

Not Steiner? ... Who, then? ... *Martin!* ... I never trusted *him* either! ... Don't worry, I'll get him in Act Two! Get yourselves a drink! I'll be right back!

He rushes off

CURTAIN

ACT II

SCENE 1

A Mountainside

The stage is bare and fully lit in dim blue. The moon is seen brightly through the UR arch. The small, wooden door in the arch UC is folded back out of sight. Music. With a loud growling, Martin, the werewolf, carries the unconscious Kitty down the aisle and up the steps onto the stage. He pauses to lift her high and let out a long howl. Cries are heard off in the foyer, and he leaps up the steps onto the high rostrum, vanishing UR. Otto, followed by D'Arcy, Steiner and Bancroft, comes down the aisle, following the werewolf's 'tracks'. All are muffled against the cold. Steiner and Otto carry lanterns. Otto, Bancroft and D'Arcy carry rifles. They climb up the steps onto the stage, Otto crossing L, the others staying C

Otto The tracks stop here. It is all rock now.

D'Arcy They can't be far in front. I think I caught a glimpse of them.

Mrs Bancroft is now making her way down the aisle. She wears her fur coat and carries an umbrella

Mrs Bancroft Hugo! D'Arcy! Where are you? Wait for me!

Bancroft We're up here, my dear. (*He helps her climb the steps up onto the stage*)

Mrs Bancroft (*grumbling*) Staggering up mountains in the middle of the night. I'm simply not cut out for it.

Bancroft I really don't know why you came, dear. This is men's work.

Mrs Bancroft I've heard men say that before—usually just as they're about to make a mess of things.

She almost collapses and Bancroft supports her

Otto We'd better rest here a moment. Here, drink this—it will warm you up. (*He comes down the steps and offers Steiner a hip-flask. He drinks*)

D'Arcy (*coming DL*) We don't have *time* for this, Inspector! Miss Bancroft is in great danger!

Bancroft I agree. You saw the state of the room she was kidnapped from. It was the work of a madman, at the very least.

Steiner (*amused*) I do assure you all the madmen are locked up this time, Bancroft. (*He proffers him the flask, and Bancroft drinks*)

D'Arcy All except the Baron. Nobody suspected *him*, did they?

Mrs Bancroft Oh come now, D'Arcy, that's a bit far-fetched. They were getting along famously. Why would *he* want to kidnap her?

D'Arcy I don't know. I just know he's the man we're looking for. (*He*

glances at the audience) I have it on very good authority. (*To Steiner*)
Forgive me, Professor. For a while, I thought it was you.

Steiner Think nothing of it. I'm accustomed to being suspected of other
people's crimes.

Bancroft What do *you* think, Inspector? Do *you* think it was the Baron?

Otto I think it was the werewolf.

Minor chords

But yes, it may also have been the Baron . . .

Minor music underlays the following

Mrs Bancroft What are you talking about, man?

Otto I am talking about the Baron *being* the werewolf.

Steiner (*contemptuously*) That's a grotesque suggestion, Inspector.

D'Arcy (*eagerly*) Not at all. Carry on, sir.

Otto I have no proof, of course, but all my life I've waited for this moment
—all my life I've watched him.

Mrs Bancroft Why?

Otto Because his mother was one.

Heavier chords

Let me tell you the story. It won't take a moment, and we need the rest.

All immediately sit, except Steiner and Otto

Bancroft Very well—go on.

Music continues to underlay

Otto It all happened 30 years ago . . . I was a child . . . the old Baron and his
Baroness were alive . . . Well, one evening the Baroness took me for a
walk in the woods . . . I had been told never to do this . . . strange things
had been happening . . . deaths among the livestock which defied explanation . . . but I was too young—I went . . . (*Brief pause*) We seemed
to walk for hours . . . and all the time it grew darker and darker—until
the full moon rose in the sky. And then—

Pause

D'Arcy Well? What happened?

Otto She changed. Right before my very eyes, she became something else—
a beast. I turned to run, and she seized my hand in her teeth . . . (*He
works the dead hand*) As you can see, most of me escaped.

Steiner How old were you at this time, Inspector?

Otto Just a few years.

Steiner Then don't you think there's another explanation?—a simpler,
more rational one? . . . That you had a nightmare, for example.

D'Arcy Pretty damn bad nightmare to wake up in the morning without
one of your feelers.

Otto Yes . . . And also, that night, something else happened . . . The
father of Ernst, the hunter, shot a wolf with a silver bullet . . . a wolf

which, when brought back to the village, turned into the shape of a woman ... the Baroness!

Heavier chords

Steiner Ridiculous.
Otto She was buried in the family plot in Walpurgisdorf Church. Although only a small boy and with a hideously wounded arm, I was taken to the funeral ... and there I saw the old Baron die of grief ... (*A sudden return of memory*) And also—there was somebody *else* there ...
Bancroft Who was it, man?
Otto I don't know. He was dressed all in black, and I didn't see his face ... But he had something to do with the horrible business—that much was obvious ... And now, nobody goes to the church any more. It is cursed.

A faint wolf-howl

Steiner I don't believe a word of it. It's pure superstition. Quite impossible.
Otto You think so. Professor? You are all alike, you men of science. If you can't weigh it, you don't believe in it. But what about heaven and hell, Professor? ... There are more things in there than are dreamt of ...

SONG: **Don't Be A Silly Sceptic**

Otto

Don't be a silly sceptic
You'll never get on
Don't be a disbeliever
It's not any fun
Just keep an open mind now
And hear everyone
Don't be a silly sceptic
You'll never get on

D'Arcy

Don't turn a deaf ear to
The sounds in the night
Bancroft
Don't turn a blind eye on
What doesn't seem right
All Three
Just keep an open mind now
And you'll see the light
Don't be a silly sceptic
You'll never get on

Otto

You have got to seek out
All the secrets all around
All Three
Don't be narrow-minded
For life is profound

One instrumental verse in which they all do a solemn little dance, including Steiner and Mrs Bancroft

All   Don't be a silly sceptic
                    You'll never get on
                    Don't be a silly sceptic
                    You'll never get on
                    Don't be a silly sceptic
                    You'll never get—aaagh!

This latter because a hideous face has appeared from DR. All recoil, and then relax as they see it is only Ingeborg, with her face lit from below by a lantern

Steiner It's all right, it's only Ingeborg.
Mrs Bancroft (*muttering*) What does he mean, *only* Ingeborg? Is there worse?
Otto What are you doing here?
Ingeborg It is Ramsey! Again he escapes!
Steiner Geblumpen Gefelte! How did it happen?
Ingeborg Not I know. My back on him turn and everything went black.
D'Arcy (*coming down C*) You mean he hit you?
Ingeborg No, he blew out the candles. Then there he is—gone!
Otto When was this?
Ingeborg One moment after you were going.
Otto Then he certainly is not responsible for Miss Bancroft's predicament.
D'Arcy Of course he isn't! I've already told you! It's your blasted Baron!

In his agitation, he jumps up the steps

Ingeborg (*scandalised*) Der Baron!
Steiner Forgive him, Ingeborg, he's a little distraught.
Mrs Bancroft (*disapprovingly*) Far *too* distraught, if you ask me!
D'Arcy (*in anguish, turning on them*) Oh, what does all this *matter*? The important thing is *Kitty*!
Bancroft Quite right, D'Arcy, I agree. We must press on.
Otto Good, But before we do so, all rifles must be reloaded with *these*.

He holds out a handful of bullets. D'Arcy and Bancroft move in to him from either side. During this, Steiner crosses quietly to Ingeborg and whispers to her

Bancroft What are those?
Otto Silver bullets. I made them from my wife's ear-rings.
Mrs Bancroft Didn't she object?
Otto (*surprised*) No, why should she?—I removed them from her ears first.
D'Arcy Come on, Professor! (*He goes up the steps to the high rostrum centre, followed by Otto*)
Steiner Coming!

He turns away from Ingeborg, who goes, as she came, Dr Bancroft has followed D'Arcy as far as the steps. Steiner crosses above Mrs Bancroft to the same place. Mrs Bancroft looks up after them dubiously

Mrs Bancroft I'm not sure I can manage it up there, Hugo. It's too steep for these heels.

D'Arcy Then we'll go on without you. Hurry up, Inspector!

D'Arcy moves to peer off through the arch, followed by Otto. Bancroft and Steiner go up the steps

Mrs Bancroft (*calling up*) He's right. You find her and hurry back. I'll make myself comfortable here.

Otto (*as they go off*) Passen Sie auf! Hier besteht Lawinengefahr!

Mrs Bancroft What did he say?

Steiner He says beware of avalanches.

Bancroft A mere exhortation. There isn't an avalanche in the world would dare envelop my wife.

D'Arcy (*off*) Come on, get schnelling, you lazy German peeler!

Bancroft We're coming, D'Arcy! Stop getting so worked up!

All exit. Mrs Bancroft makes herself comfortable, sitting on downstage edge of the steps LC. She takes out a thermos flask and helps herself to coffee. Gentle music. After a moment, Ramsey appears from the arch entrance, his shirt still covered in blood. He sees her, smiles secretively, and creeps down to behind her. He slowly reaches out a hand towards her throat, and then touches her on the shoulder. She gives a terrible shriek, leaps in the air, turns and smashes him over the head with her umbrella

Mrs Bancroft Brute! (*She hits him again and again, forcing him to the ground*) You great bully! Just because you're a man and I'm a defence-less woman! . . . (*As she hits him*) Help! Help! I'm being attacked! Help!

Ramsey I'd help you if I could.

Mrs Bancroft (*still hitting him*) Don't talk to me, you swaggering great hooligan! I'd show you a thing or two if I wasn't a frail female!

Ramsey Alliterative but inaccurate, madam.

She pauses in her attack

Mrs Bancroft What did you say?

Ramsey I promulgated the proposition that your terminal expostulation was constructed alliteratively and inaccurately, madam.

Mrs Bancroft That was not only insulting, it was almost lucid. (*Suspiciously*) Are you sure you're round the twist?

Ramsey Oh, I have an occasional transitory rationality. (*He howls like a wolf*) Of course, its only occasional and transitory.

Distant howl of a wolf. Ramsey draws himself up and howls louder

There. *That* gave him a piece of my mind.

Mrs Bancroft Who?

Ramsey The pack-leader. He's been getting a bit too big for his paws lately. Have a piece of rabbit.

He offers her a bloody piece of bone

Mrs Bancroft (*shuddering*) No, thank you.

He shrugs and chews it himself

What have you done with my daughter?

Ramsey What does she say I did with her?

Mrs Bancroft We can't find her.

Ramsey Then we'd better look for her.

Mrs Bancroft (*suspiciously*) Why?

Ramsey We can ask her what I did with her.

Mrs Bancroft But she's been kidnapped—we're not sure by whom.

Ramsey What.

Mrs Bancroft What?

Ramsey Not whom.

Mrs Bancroft What?

Ramsey That's right. What. By *what* has she been kidnapped. Well, *I* know, and I'm the only one who does. I've been studying him.

Mrs Bancroft (*totally bemused*) What?

Ramsey That's the fellow.

Mrs Bancroft (*grimly*) I'm going to hit you with my umbrella in a minute.

Ramsey You've already hit me with your umbrella.

Mrs Bancroft I was just practising.

Ramsey Seemed perfect to me.

Mrs Bancroft One can always improve.

Ramsey Then we'd better go. Follow me.

Mrs Bancroft For what?

Ramsey That's right. He'll be there. He always takes them to the same place.

Mrs Bancroft He?

Ramsey *It!* Sorry—my fault, that time. *It* always takes them to the same place. Every full moon. Well, hurry up. Don't just stand there.

Mrs Bancroft You haven't moved yourself yet.

Ramsey (*surprised*) I haven't? (*Looks at his feet*) You're right. I must have been standing still. Off you go, then. *I*'ll follow *you*.

Mrs Bancroft But I don't know where we're going!

Ramsey Just do as I do.

He creeps UL. She shrugs and follows him. He puts finger to his lips, shushes her and beckons her to follow him up onto the high rostrum and out UR. Grumbling under her breath, she follows him. Cross-fade lighting to the next scene

SCENE 2

A Cave

Loud growling heard. Light collects dimly in the area below the high rostrum, at stage level. A faint blue glow from the special inside the rostrum spills through the small arch. Martin comes through this arch, carrying the unconscious Kitty. He lays her down. He looks down at her, cocking his head

*from side to side, a deep, low, enquiring rumble in his throat (offstage micro-
phone). He holds out a hand to touch her neck. Faint shouts are heard*

D'Arcy (*off—very faint indeed*) Miss Bancroft? . . . Miss Bancroft? . . .

*With a snarl, the werewolf goes back to the UC arch, pauses in it, looks
back at the unconscious Kitty, then goes out. There is a loud grating sound
and the dim blue glow from within the arch is blotted out. A pause, and
then Kitty sits up*

Kitty Where am I? (*She looks around her*) It seems to be some sort of cave.
(*She rises and goes to the UC arch, and looks off through it*) It's blocked
off! I'm trapped! (*She moves back slowly C, as her memory comes back*)
Oh, that awful face! . . . What was it? . . . *Who* was it? . . . It was so
horrible, and yet—somehow, it seemed strangely familiar . . .

*There is a sudden wolf-howl, off. She shrieks, then forces herself to keep
calm*

No . . . mustn't give in . . . Martin will come for me soon . . . I know he
will . . . (*She lowers herself slowly, and sits on the floor*) It's just that I do
so hate being on my own! . . .

*In sitting, she becomes aware of the penny whistle, which she still carries on
her. She takes it out, and looks at it almost fondly. In an attempt to cheer
herself up, she blows a little phrase. The piano replies, lower down the scale.
She listens, then tries again. Once more, the piano replies. She plays a third
time, and the piano follows, going into tempo*

SONG: I Like A Lot Of Friends

Kitty   I hate to be here just with me
       Cos I'm poor company
       I like a lot of friends around
       I hate to be so solitary
       So Open Sesame
       And let me hear a cheerful sound

She rises

       But I won't let it get me
       I'll fight it with a song
       No, I won't let it fret me
       I know I'll get along

       I hate to be here just with me
       Cos I'm poor company
       I like a lot of friends around

*But she has remembered where she is, and finishes gloomily, sinking to her
knees once more. There is a grating sound, and the blue glow appears in the
arch once more. Unseen by her, the werewolf appears behind her. It comes
down slowly behind her, lifting its claws, as if to pounce on her . . . But as it
does so, she blows a phrase on the whistle and is answered by the piano. The*

werewolf pauses. She blows a second phrase and the piano answers it. The werewolf is charmed. She and the piano play together, in tempo, and she sings once more, this time dancing as well. At first, the werewolf scratches its head, but then—completely charmed and captivated by the music—it dances behind her, mimicking her steps

> I hate to be here just with me
> It's not my kind of scene
> I like a lot of pals as well
> I hate to be so solitary
> You know just what I mean
> I'd like to wave it all farewell
>
> But I won't let it shake me
> I'll fight it with a song
> No, I won't let it break me
> I know I'll get along
>
> I hate to be here just with me
> Cos I'm poor company
> I like a lot of friends around
> I like a lot of friends a—aaaagh!

Turning in the dance, she sees the werewolf and screams. Immediately, it loses its good humour, and growls thunderously, closing in on her. She plays a note on the whistle. It calms. She continues playing, the werewolf purring and grunting happily, trying to dance a little jig. She keeps playing, edging around as she does so. Unfortunately, unable to play and see where she is going at the same time, she trips over the step and falls, the whistle rolling to the ground. Once more, the spell is broken, but this time—before she can reach out and pick it up—the werewolf pounces on the whistle, and bites it to pieces in its teeth. Kitty gets to her knees and backs off. The werewolf begins to advance on her, growling horribly. She dodges through its legs, and past, running for the arch, but the werewolf is too quick for her, and gets there first. She runs UR and jumps on to the bench, climbing up onto the high rostrum, but the werewolf chases her, and pulls her down. She kicks it in the groin, and in almost comically surprised pain it rolls away from her—unfortunately in front of the entrance. She tries to run past it to UL, but it reaches out a hand, holds an ankle and she trips and falls. It gathers itself and advances on her. She crawls backwards, as it towers over her. But—as it is about to spring on her and tear her throat out—Ramsey rushes on through the UC archway, and flings himself on to the werewolf's back

Ramsey Wait!

The werewolf turns round and round, trying to dislodge him. Mrs Bancroft rushes in through the arch. She calls across

Mrs Bancroft Kitty!

Kitty runs across to her mother. The werewolf dislodges Ramsey, flings him to the ground, jumps on him and quickly tears his throat out, Ramsey screaming. He gives a quick howl, then turns to the two women. He advances to the edge of the steps. Suddenly, Steiner runs in through the archway, carrying a lantern. He holds it in the werewolf's face, and it backs off, growling

Steiner Behind me, for your lives!

He forces the werewolf towards the stairs to the higher rostrum

D'Arcy (*off*) Where have you got to, Professor?
Kitty (*screaming*) Here, D'Arcy! In here!

D'Arcy rushes in through the arch, still carrying his rifle

D'Arcy Good God! Let me get a shot at it!

The werewolf leaps on to the table above the DL entrance, reaches up, opens a small trap high in the wall, and wriggles through. While it is doing this, D'Arcy is trying to get a shot at it, but Steiner has backed and impedes him— seemingly accidentally

Damn it, Steiner! Get out of the way!

As Bancroft and Otto rush in the UC arch, D'Arcy pushes Steiner out of the way, and fires at the werewolf—the rifle making a tremendous bang—but it is too late—the ledge is empty, the werewolf gone. D'Arcy rushes across, climbs onto the table and peers into the hole. Bancroft goes to the two women. Otto almost dances with excitement

Otto Did you *see* it? Did you *see* it?
Bancroft Yes, yes, we all saw it. (*Holding onto Kitty*) Kitty!
Kitty Daddy!
Mrs Bancroft What on earth was it?
Otto (*triumphantly, to Steiner*) Well, Professor?
Steiner (*reluctantly*) It was a werewolf. It seems incredible. Otto, I owe you an apology. Heaven and Hell are more densely populated than I thought.
Bancroft And I owe *you* one, Konrad. If you hadn't acted so promptly, that devilish thing would have killed my daughter.
Mrs Bancroft You're not forgetting *me*, I hope, Hugo?
Kitty No, Mother, it would have killed all of us . . . (*She crosses L to the steps*) Just as it killed poor Mr Ramsey.

Soft music as she kneels by him. D'Arcy turns to her and moves to kneel by him

He seemed to know about the thing somehow. (*She picks up the battered whistle*) And he was right—this was very soothing.
Steiner Well, he's at rest now, poor fellow.
Otto And now I must ask you all . . . The wolf man . . . Did anybody recognise who it might have been?
Mrs Bancroft What? Recognise? That? I shouldn't have thought so.
Kitty No, it was far too horrid.
D'Arcy Oh no, it wasn't. I got a good look at it. And I know who it was. It was the Baron.

Steiner The Baron?

Mrs Bancroft Don't be absurd, D'Arcy. You're talking about a continental gentleman.

D'Arcy (*to Otto*) Well, Inspector? You saw him too.

Otto (*slowly*) It could have been. I'm not sure.

D'Arcy What do you mean, you're not sure? Just now you said you'd suspected him all your life!

Otto Yes, but I'm a policeman: I need evidence.

D'Arcy Why? You're a *German* policeman, aren't you? . . . And I tell you it was *him!*

Kitty (*rising and moving RC*) How *could* you, D'Arcy! You know my feelings for Martin—for the Baron—and yet you concoct this hideous story! It's too bad of you!

D'Arcy But Miss Bancroft, I tell you I'm *sure*—

Kitty Well, *I*'m sure too, D'Arcy! Quite sure that I never want to see you again! (*To Bancroft*) Take me home, Daddy.

Mrs Bancroft Yes.

Bancroft No.

Mrs Bancroft (*staring at him in amazement*) No? Did you say 'No', Hugo? I could have sworn you said 'No'.

Bancroft Then your swearer's in tip-top condition, my dear. We can't leave this thing now—simply because *our* daughter's safe. There are *other people's* daughters to consider. We must continue the chase!

Major music underlays

Otto Well said, Doctor! You are right! We must track him down—whoever he is—track him down and destroy him. Are you with us, D'Arcy?

D'Arcy looks at Kitty. She turns her back on him and crosses in front of Bancroft to her mother. He sighs, then straightens his back determinedly

D'Arcy Yes, I am. (*He turns back to the table*) Give me a leg up, and I'll have a recce.

He climbs on to the table. Otto crosses and helps him as he clambers up and peers through the hole

Steiner (*coming down the steps to C*) I shall return with the ladies. We can't let them go home by themselves.

Bancroft Good thinking, Konrad. (*Turning to the women*) Go with him, my dears. You'll be quite safe. And don't worry about us. We may be gone some little time. (*He turns and moves to D'Arcy and Otto*)

Steiner moves up to the arch, waiting for the women

Mrs Bancroft Good luck, Hugo! (*To Steiner*) Lead on, Professor.

Steiner goes out through the UC arch, followed by Mrs Bancroft. Kitty pauses to call across to D'Arcy

Kitty You'll see how wrong you are, D'Arcy! You'll see . . . and then you'll be sorry!

She goes out UC. Light in the area R fades, concentrating on D'Arcy, Otto and Bancroft

Otto Can you make out where it goes to?
D'Arcy On up through the mountain. It's a fault—a kind of chimney. Are you game to climb it, gentlemen?
Bancroft We're more than game. Lead on, my boy.
Otto We're right behind you.

As D'Arcy climbs through, fade to BLACKOUT. *Piano plays a short, exciting bridge into the next scene*

Scene 3

Walpurgisdorf Castle

During the BLACKOUT, *the chair has been reset as before, and the small wooden door fitted back into the arch UC. A tray with drinks has been placed on the table above the DL entrance. Loud growling and snarling is heard, off, as the lights rise on the scene. The cyclorama is dim and blue, with no moon visible. Ingeborg backs on through the small arch UC, beating back something we can't see*

Ingeborg Back! ... Get back!

She pulls the door closed, having to use all her strength, since whatever is snarling on the other side of it is trying to heave it open. Eventually, she shoots home a bolt and relaxes, mopping her brow

I need a drink. A large big drink.

She crosses to the table. As she mounts the step, she pauses

Why am I speaking English? (*Shrugging*) Oh well, it's cheaper than sub-titles.

As she pours herself a drink, there is a loud growling, off, and a crash against the small door. She shouts

Shut up! What's the matter with you? Where do you think you are? This is Walpurgisdorf! *Enjoy* it! ... *I* do.

SONG: **Walpurgisdorf**

Ingeborg   When you're living in Walpurgisdorf
You may ...
... be aware of things both odd and eerie
People disappear
Quite a few go every year
Still, there's lots left in Walpurgisdorf

Walpurgis ... dorf is bliss
Walpurgisdorf I should miss

When you're working in Walpurgisdorf
Don't be . . .
. . . frightened by those strange uncanny whispers
Noises in the night
Could be fright or sheer delight
Can't be choosy in Walpurgisdorf

Walpurgis . . . dorf is bliss
Walpurgisdorf I could kiss

When you're strolling in Walpurgisdorf
You can . . .
. . . walk and wander everywhere so safely
Just go out in fives
Load your guns and bring your knives
Maybe you'll survive Walpurgisdorf

Walpurgis . . . dorf is bliss
Walpurgisdorf I should miss

When you're sleeping in Walpurgisdorf
You may . . .
. . . scream in bed and suffer awful nightmares
Well, don't sweat and fret
You ain't got to sleep just yet
It's no dream—it's just Walpurgisdorf
Oh no . . .
It's no dream— it's just Walpurgisdorf

Walpurgis . . .
Walpurgis . . .
Walpurgis . . .

Steiner comes in DL, with Mrs Bancroft and Kitty

Steiner Wait for me in the study, Ingeborg. There are a few things I wish to discuss with you.
Ingeborg Zu Befehl. (*She goes*)
Steiner You'll excuse me, of course, Mrs Bancroft. Help yourself to a drink.
Mrs Bancroft Not just yet, if you don't mind.
Steiner As you wish. (*He goes*)
Mrs Bancroft I'm going to my room, Kitty. Are you coming?
Kitty In a moment, Mummy. I want to think for a while.
Mrs Bancroft Very well. I shall go and change and join you later.

She goes. Left alone, Kitty wanders absently running her hands over the back of the chair. Silence, at first, and then a faint scratching sound from the door in the arch. Kitty turns and looks at it. The scratching turns into a low knocking. Minor chords on the piano. Kitty goes slowly to the door, listens at it, puzzled. Knocking grows louder. Crescendo in the music. Slowly, Kitty draws back the bolt in the door, opens it and peers inside. She steps back L, with a cry. Brief pause—and Martin comes out

Martin My dear Kitty. (*He embraces her*)

Kitty Oh Martin, I've been so frightened without you!

Martin There there, it's all over now. Come and sit down. (*He leads her to the chair*)

Kitty You've no idea how horrid it was. There was this *thing*—this monster!

Martin Yes, I've heard all about it. It must have been terrible for you. (*He sits her in the chair and crouches beside her*)

Kitty And *D'Arcy*! . . . Do you know what D'Arcy said? He said it was *you*!

Martin (*incredulously*) Amazing! Jealousy will make a man say almost anything.

Kitty Yes, but—Martin—where *were* you?

Martin What do you mean?

Kitty Well, after I was abducted, Mummy said they looked all over for you.

Martin (*rising, turning away from her*) I was out in the forest. A new pack has moved into the area. I was studying it.

Kitty (*a little coldly*) Oh. I see.

Martin You surely don't think I'd have abandoned you? If only I'd *known*—!

Kitty doesn't reply, sulking prettily

I suppose that damned butler rescued you again?

Kitty Well, he did have a hand in it.

Martin (*muttering furiously*) Zum Teufel mit dem mann!

Kitty Why, Martin, didn't you *want* me to be rescued?

Martin (*kneeling beside her*) Why, yes, of course. He is a brave, wonderful man—and I am behaving like a child.

Kitty (*melting now that he is close*) Oh no, Martin—not like a child—not like a *child*, Martin . . . (*She closes her eyes and lifts her face to be kissed, but Martin abruptly rises, leaves her, goes and looks off DL*)

Martin It's a beautiful night.

Kitty (*fed up*) It is from *here*, yes. It's not so beautiful when you're out in the middle of it, being threatened by some kind of hairy hobgoblin.

Martin (*his mind far away*) It must have been terrible for you. Do you know there's a full moon?

Kitty (*angrily*) Well, it's *round*, so I suppose it's *full*! . . .

Minor music underlays the following

Martin I'll open the doors . . . You'll see it more clearly.

He reaches off. Sound of doors opening. Thin whistle of wind

Kitty I don't *want* to see it clearly. I've *seen* it! . . . Martin, it's *cold*! (*He ignores her, staring off raptly, his face lit by moonlight*) Talk about dampening a young girl's ardour . . . Martin, it's *freezing*!

Martin begins to pant heavily. Kitty rises

Martin, please! What's the matter with you?

She moves a little towards him. He turns towards her—an evil expression on his face. He makes a move towards her, and Steiner comes on suddenly

Steiner Martin!

He hurries across L, reaches out. Sound of door being closed. The wind dies. The moonlight is cut off. The music stops

Martin I was just letting in some air . . . It's very stuffy in here.
Steiner I expect you're feeling tired.
Martin What? . . . Oh yes, that must be it. (*He rubs his head vaguely*)
Steiner Martin, Miss Bancroft is in a state of shock. She needs peace and quiet. I'd rather you left her at the moment.
Martin Of course. (*To Kitty*) My apologies. I'm . . . tired . . . as the Professor says. I'll go to my quarters. (*He crosses towards the small door*)
Kitty Will I see you later?
Martin Possibly. For the moment, however, I must go and . . . change . . . change into something more comfortable. Excuse me. (*He goes quickly through the small door*)
Kitty I really must thank you, Professor, for looking after me so awfully well.

Steiner wanders casually to the small door

Steiner Think nothing of it, my dear. (*He casually shoots the bolt home without Kitty seeing it*) You are quite safe now . . . with me.

Fade to BLACKOUT

SCENE 4

Walpurgisdorf Church

Dim moonlight on the high UR rostrum area. The moon shines brightly. Owl hoots are heard, followed by muffled voices, below the rostrum

Bancroft (*off*) D'Arcy! That's my *head* you're treading on!
D'Arcy (*off*) Sorry, Sir, I thought it was a rock.
Otto (*off*) Scheisse!
D'Arcy (*off*) Now what?
Otto (*off*) That's *my* head.
D'Arcy (*off*) Well, I've got to get a toe-hold somewhere. This blasted chimney just goes on up and up and up.

A dull clonk

Ow!

Otto
Bancroft⎫ (*together*) What's that?

D'Arcy (*off*) *My* head. We seem to have come to a dead end.

A creaking sound. The grave-trap shifts slightly

Wait a minute. I think it's loose!

The grave-trap moves again, grating

Yes, by George, it's a kind of lid! Come on—all together!

The grave-trap is lifted up and falls back with a crash. The heads of Otto, Bancroft and D'Arcy appear in the grave, Otto to the R, D'Arcy to the L. They look around

Otto Mein Gott! Gott O Gott!

Bancroft We're in a grave.

D'Arcy It's unoccupied, I hope?

Otto Well, it *was*.

Bancroft Don't be ridiculous. It's some kind of secret passageway. But to *where*? Where are we?

Otto I think *I* can answer that, gentlemen . . . This is the old church of Walpurgisdorf, on the mountain . . .

Minor chords

The one in which I saw the Baron's mother buried all those years ago, as a little boy.

D'Arcy Is this her grave?

Otto Yes.

D'Arcy Then—if this is her grave—and you saw her buried—what became of her body?

Otto I don't care to think about it. Wolves are scavengers too, you know. (*He climbs out and offers his hand to Bancroft*) Let me assist you, Doctor. (*He helps Bancroft out. D'Arcy clambers out on his own*) One thing I *do* know—(*He breaks off as he finds that his dead hand is locked around Bancroft's and, after a considerable struggle, frees it*)—this tunnel did not exist then. Her body was properly buried. I saw it myself.

D'Arcy Then we must be careful. That devilish thing can't be far away. (*He heaves the grave-trap shut again*)

Otto Perhaps. On the other hand, it took us hours to climb that damned chimney.

Bancroft That's one of the disadvantages of not being a werewolf, I suppose.

D'Arcy All the same, I suggest we search the graveyard—and carefully. Cock your pieces, gentlemen.

Bancroft I beg your pardon?

D'Arcy demonstrates on his rifle

Oh, I see. (*He and Otto cock the rifles' actions*)

D'Arcy You go that way, Doctor. (*He indicates UR arch*) Inspector, you check inside the church. (*He indicates UR entrance*) I'll look around here.

They turn to go, but Bancroft stops suddenly

Bancroft Wait a minute. (*To Otto*) Didn't you say something about this place being haunted?

Otto Yes, the ghost of an old priest roams here. I have seen it myself.

Bancroft That's nice. And suppose we bump into him tonight?
Otto Shoot him with your silver bullets.
Bancroft I thought they only worked on werewolves?
Otto They do, but I don't want you worried.
D'Arcy (*impatiently*) Oh stop quibbling, and get on with the search. We haven't got all night.

Otto creeps off through UR entrance. Bancroft goes through UR arch and off R. D'Arcy prowls around the rostrum area, rifle at the ready, searching, occasionally jumping at shadows

Nothing. (*He sits on the edge of the rostrum L, dejectedly*) Oh, it's no use. I can't concentrate. All I can think about is Kitty and that damn smooth villain who's got her twisted around his little finger—or rather, his little *claw*, if my suspicions are correct . . . I should have introduced myself properly at the outset—at least that old bag of a mother of hers would have been on my side—an English Lord outranks a Prussian Baron any day of the week. Oh, how difficult love is! No wonder the poor child's confused! . . .

SONG: **Lovers Can't Agree**

D'Arcy   Love is so blind
          We never seem to see
          The way that things are meant to be
          Love's in the mind
          Or so it seems to me
          And that's why lovers can't agree

          It's such a sad state of affairs
          We're always caught so unawares

          Love is so blind
          We never seem to see
          The way that things are meant to be

          Love isn't kind
          It hides away the key
          It makes a fool of you and me
          Love is designed
          To be a mystery
          And that's why lovers can't agree

          It's such a strange game that we play
          We throw those chances away

The old Pastor appears from UL entrance and regards him in astonishment
          Love is so blind
          We never seem to see
          The way that things are meant to be

The old Pastor creeps up the steps behind him and proceeds to haunt him—but D'Arcy is too deep in his own thoughts to notice

Pastor Woo! . . . (*No response. He tries again*) Woo! . . . (*No response. He tries again—much louder*) Woo! . . .

D'Arcy leaps to his feet with a yell, backs a little, and aims his rifle at the Pastor who promptly throws himself flat

Don't shoot, Sir, don't shoot! I wouldn't have haunted you if I'd known you were armed! Its only old Schneidhuber the Pastor, Sir. He means no harm. He's a man of the church, Sir. At least, he *was*, until some dumpkopf desecrated it.
D'Arcy (*shouting off*) Inspector! . . . Doctor Bancroft!

They rush back on, staring at the Pastor. N.B. Since the Pastor is now speaking English, he speaks with a German accent

Otto Lieber Gott!
Bancroft Who is it?
D'Arcy He *says* he's somebody called Pastor Schneidhuber.
Otto It's *true*! It *is* old Schneidhuber! He was Pastor here over thirty years ago! No wonder we thought we had a ghost.

He crosses in front of D'Arcy and bends over the Pastor

Well, old man. Do you recognise *me* after all this time?
Pastor (*rising*) Yes. You were that horrible sneaky child with the overbearing officious manner and the talent for telling tales. Whatever became of you?
Otto I became Chief of Police.
Pastor God is good.
Otto (*looking the Pastor up and down*) And may one enquire what *you* have been doing here all these years?
Pastor Living like a hermit—what else? People think I'm a ghost. I don't disillusion them, poor credulous fools. Besides, when they run away they drop things—food and such. It's been most useful.
Otto So! Impersonating a ghost! You'll get life for that.
D'Arcy Just a moment. Tell me, Pastor, you haven't seen a werewolf here, by any chance, have you?
Pastor A werewolf? (*Thoughtfully*) A *werewolf*? . . .
Bancroft You couldn't miss him. He's got hair all over his face, little red eyes, and teeth down to his chin.
Pastor Oh, *that* werewolf!
D'Arcy Then you've seen him?
Pastor No . . . not recently.
Otto When then?
Pastor It's difficult to be sure. One night's very like another up here.
D'Arcy But do you think you'd recognise him if you saw him again?
Pastor I might. But these werewolves, they all look the same to me.
Otto Tell me something else, Pastor . . .
Pastor Yes?
Otto Cast your mind back thirty years, to the funeral of the old Baroness.

There was a man standing *there*—(*indicating DR*)—a man dressed in
black.
Pastor Oh yes, *him*. (*Shaking his head*) Dreadful business.
D'Arcy Why do you say that?
Pastor I can't remember. I know I said it at the time.
Otto Who was it?
Pastor I can't remember. It was so long ago. I think he was a cousin of the
family.
Otto Interesting. Very interesting.
D'Arcy I don't see why. We *know* who we're looking for. It's Martin von
Heilmann—and he must have been a *baby* thirty years ago!
Otto Well, I hope so. I hope it's that simple.
Bancroft (*suddenly*) Good heavens, look at *this*!

*During the preceding, he has been glancing casually down at the grave-trap.
Now, he points at it dramatically. All cluster by the trap, peering down at it*

D'Arcy What is it?
Bancroft (*pointing*) *There*, look! Read what it says!
Otto (*reading*) "Einwig Holstein, Stone-Mason."
Bancroft (*impatiently*) No, not there! *There*, look!
Otto (*reading*) "Here lie the mortal remains of Baroness Sophie von
Heilmann" . . . Well, what about it? We know this.

Bancroft Read *on*, man, read *on*!

Otto reads silently and reacts. D'Arcy does the same

Otto Mein Gott!
D'Arcy My God!
Otto Gott in Himmel!
D'Arcy God in Heaven!
Otto (*irritably*) I know what I mean, D'Arcy, stop translating me! . . .
"Born Steiner!" That's what it says—"Baroness Sophie von Heilmann,
born Steiner!"

Heavy minor chords

So! *He*'s the cousin! *He*'s the man in black! How could I have been
so blind?
Bancroft Can we be sure?
Otto What other explanation is there? Whether or no he is a shape-
shifter himself, I don't know—but he's certainly got something to do
with this business!
Pastor (*who has been searching his memory*) Steiner! . . . I think I remember
him now. He left the village to study medicine, I believe.
Otto No! To let the heat die down! And twenty years later, when it's all
forgotten, he returns! Who recognises him after all this time? Nobody!
Not even me!
Bancroft (*to the Pastor*) Could you identify this Steiner as your man in
black, do you think, Pastor?

Pastor I might. But these men in black, they all look the same to me. It's possible.

Bancroft Then you'd better come with us.

D'Arcy Yes, and quickly. There's no time to lose. (*He has an awful thought*) Good God! We put Kitty into his care!

Bancroft And my wife!

Otto Then perhaps they're safe.

D'Arcy We can't take that chance! We must hurry back!

Bancroft What, all the way back down that damned hole? It'll take hours again!

Otto No! I know a better way! Follow me! We must get across to the ski-run!

He hurries out through the arch UR. The others follow him

D'Arcy Come on, Pastor!

Pastor (*as they go*) Oh dear, I wish I hadn't tried to haunt you now!

Bancroft (*the last to go*) Tell me, why does everybody speak such damned good English around here?

Cross-fade lighting to downstage area for the next scene

SCENE 5

Walpurgisdorf Castle

The moon is huge and bright through the UL arch now. Steiner and Kitty are as we last saw them. Mrs Bancroft comes on

Mrs Bancroft Now then, Professor, I think I'll take you up on that kind offer of a drink. It's been a very trying day.

Steiner By all means. Ingeborg!

Ingeborg appears swiftly and silently behind Mrs Bancroft

Gib Frau Bancroft was zu trinken . . .

Ingeborg goes to the table

(*as Ingeborg passes*) . . . etwas besonderes.

Ingeborg Sofort. (*She glides to the table—Kitty looks off left*)

Kitty It's beginning to snow. I do hope Daddy's going to be all right.

Mrs Bancroft (*crossing to put an arm round her*) Don't worry, dear, he'll be quite safe with D'Arcy.

Kitty (*scornfully*) Oh, *him*.

Mrs Bancroft He's useless as a servant, but he does seem to have *some* qualities . . .

Behind them, Ingeborg is mixing a drink. She stirs it with a spoon, then hurriedly hides the spoon when she discovers that the bowl has melted and the handle is twisted and black. She gives the drink to Mrs Bancroft, unable to restrain an evil smile

Ingeborg Ihr Getränk, meine Dame.

Mrs Bancroft Oh, thank you. (*She drains it*) Tasted a bit medicinal, but otherwise—(*She clutches her throat, chokes, collapses*)

Kitty goes down with her, supporting her

Kitty Mother! What's happened? (*To Ingeborg*) What have you done to her?

Steiner (*crossing L to them*) Nothing serious. I've just given her a few knock-out drops, that is all. I can't have her interfering with my plans, can I?

Kitty (*wildly*) Plans? What plans?

Steiner (*to Ingeborg*) Pack sie! An den stuhl fesseln!

Ingeborg Zu Befehl! (*She grabs Kitty, dragging her, struggling, to her feet*)

Kitty Martin! Martin!

A thud on the other side of the small door

Steiner Don't worry, my dear—your lover Martin will soon be with you . . . soon . . . very soon!

He laughs madly. A hysterical scratching and growling from the other side of the door. The lighting immediately cross-cuts to the high UR rostrum

SCENE 6

A Mountainside

During the preceding scene, the grave-trap has been opened quietly, and a blocking rostrum placed below it. We discover Otto, D'Arcy, Bancroft and the Pastor standing up to their shins in the trap, all carrying ski sticks, and miming a mad ski dash downhill from R to L, their rifles strapped to their backs. An effects projector projects snow onto the cyclorama seen through the arch UR. Sound of wind and sliding skis

Otto (*shouting*) Is better than walking, ja?

Bancroft Well, it's certainly a damn sight quicker! That is, if we don't kill ourselves first!

Pastor Don't say it! I'm too old to die!

D'Arcy (*pointing ahead with a ski stick*) Look! I can see the lights of the village below us!

Bancroft What do we do when we get to the bottom? Walk? It's still a devil of a long way!

Otto Don't worry—I have another little trick up my sleeve yet.

Loud wolf-howling

Pastor Don't look now, but I think we're being followed!

Otto (*looking back*) Wolves! *Real* wolves, this time! Ski faster! Ski faster! (*He draws his pistol and fires two shots behind him*)

D'Arcy Save your energy, Inspector! It's just a waste of good silver! Put your heads down and *ski*!

Cross-cut lighting immediately to DL area

SCENE 7

Walpurgisdorf Castle

During the preceding scene, a chair looking like a dentist's operating chair has been wheeled on quietly to C in the DL rostrum area, and Kitty strapped into it. Nearby has been wheeled an instruments trolley, with a tray on it in which is a hypodermic syringe. Steiner has donned a green operating gown, complete with big rubber gloves, rubber boots, and a little light in the centre of his forehead. Ingeborg is completing tying Mrs Bancroft to the bench below the DL entrance, and gagging her. She splutters furiously

Steiner Silence, woman! If your husband had any sense, he would have done this years ago! (*To Kitty*) And now . . . we can begin.

Kitty Begin *what*?

Steiner A little experiment, my dear. You have the privilege of partici-
pating in a unique historic moment. Tonight, all my life's hard labour is going to come to fruition. You see, I have for many long years now been studying lycanthropy—a mental condition in which the patient thinks himself to be an animal—usually a wolf. But *I* had always known it to be more than a mere mental condition . . . because some thirty years ago I actually saw a woman change into a wolf! . . . But how to recreate that metamorphosis! That was the question that burned itself into my soul! . . . Ah, how many sleepless night have I spent, how many candles burnt at both ends, seeking an answer to the problem! . . . And then, one day, I *saw* it! It was so simple! . . . Instead of seeking to cure my patients, I encouraged them to live out their fantasies to the full . . . And it worked! . . . It *worked*! . . . Imagine my excitement when, one day, before my very eyes, one of my patients actually *changed*! . . . The beast was there! . . . Not a mere figment of the imagination, but a fact! . . .

Loud growling from the other side of the small door

There! You can hear one now! Your good friend, Martin.

Kitty No!

Steiner Yes. Martin is a werewolf.

Heavy minor chords

The only question left is whether a werewolf can be *bred*—whether the condition is truly hereditary . . . You see, it was Martin's mother I first saw change some thirty years ago . . . (*He reminisces*) Ah, she was a delightful woman! I became her consort for a while. She had a mar-
vellous flair for—but that's another story . . . Suffice it to say that Martin is my creation in more ways than one.

Kitty You don't mean—?

Minor chords

Steiner Yes. Martin is my son.

Kitty (*struggling desperately*) Why are you doing this? What can you hope to achieve?

Steiner What can I hope to achieve? I hope—no!—I *shall* achieve—the creation of an entirely new species ... *Lupus Steinerii*! ... And you, my dear, you will be the first mother of my new species—(*pinching her cheek in ecstasy*) Lucky girl! ... (*More serious*) I had intended that slut Frau Gessler to be the first mother—but she was a failure—she enjoyed the condition too much—I couldn't control her. However, I doubt there will be any such trouble with you, my dear. (*With great meaning*) Ingeborg —the hypodermic needle.

Ingeborg brings hypodermic needle from the table. Loud growling from behind the small door

Listen to your lover, my dear! He can scarce contain himself! ... Though I hope he does, otherwise we shall have to call off the experiment and come back again tomorrow night.

Kitty (*desperately*) But there's nothing wrong with me! There's nothing to —breed! I don't *have* lycanthropy!

Steiner But my dear, you forget my enormous discovery. *Nobody is normal!* ... Oh yes, you have it somewhere. We *all* have it somewhere. (*He takes the syringe from Ingeborg and holds it before his eyes*) The only question ... How to find the key that unlocks the gate ... (*He approaches her with the syringe. Loud growling from the small door. The lighting* immediately *cross-cuts to the high UR rostrum*

SCENE 8

A Road

During this scene, although unlit, Steiner, Kitty, Ingeborg and Mrs Bancroft remain frozen. During the preceding scene a colourful profile depicting the side of a sled has been added to the front of the grave-trap. We discover Otto, Bancroft, the Pastor and D'Arcy sitting in the sled as if travelling from R to L. Otto holds short reins and cracks a long whip. An effects projector projects snow on to the cyclorama seen through the UR arch. Sound of thudding hooves, neighing horses, jingling sleigh-bells against a background of wind

D'Arcy Hurry up, Inspector! We must get there in time!

Otto (*whipping*) We can't go any faster! My arm's getting tired, as it is!

Loud wolf-howling

Bancroft (*looking back*) Oh my God, those wolves! They're gaining on us!

D'Arcy Leave them to me! (*D'Arcy fires behind him with the rifle, through the UR entrance*) Curses! Missed! Can't see a thing in this blasted snow!

A loud snarling and a wolf's head appears through the UR entrance, swinging from side to side as if running fast. D'Arcy fires at it. A loud yelp, the head reacts upwards and falls back through the entrance

Got one of the brutes!

Another loud snarling, and a second head appears—actually the same one, of course. D'Arcy is busy reloading

Bancroft (*in panic*) D'Arcy!

D'Arcy completes reloading and shoots the wolf. Same pantomime as before, followed by a loud snarling from several throats

Otto You've got the leader!
D'Arcy They're stopping to eat it! The filthy brutes, they're tearing one another to pieces!
Pastor Well, at least we're in the clear now!
Bancroft (*pointing front*) Look out!

Otto hauls in the reins—too late. A loud crash and all are thrown forward. They climb out quickly and examine the sled

Otto We've run into a tree!
D'Arcy The runners are gone!
Bancroft Then we'll have to make the rest of the way on foot! Come on! Run!

Lighting immediately cross-cuts to DL area

SCENE 9

Walpurgisdorf Castle

Steiner and Ingeborg are intently watching Kitty after her injection. Loud growling from behind the small door, and a crash against it

Steiner (*not looking*) Patience, Martin. Have patience. She will soon be ready ... (*To Kitty*) And now, my dear ... (*He takes a silver fob-watch from his waistcoat and swings it before her eyes. Eerie, tinkling music on the piano*) Look at this little bauble ... See how it shines ... Look deep into it ... deep ... Now tell me, what does it say to you? ... What does it say?
Kitty Half-past twelve.
Steiner (*furious*) No! No, you dumpkopf! It says my eylids are heavy! It says I can't keep my eyes open! This is no time for reality! Just sit there with your mouth open and your mind empty! It should be easy for you!—you're *English*, aren't you? (*He tries again, swinging the watch. The music continues*) Now, sleep ... sleep ... sleep ...
Kitty How can I sleep with that piano playing all the time?

Steiner casts up his eyes, goes and swings the watch in front of the pianist's eyes

Steiner I will not play the piano, Ian (*or whatever his name is*) ... I will not play the piano ...

The piano stops. Steiner returns to Kitty and swings the watch

Sleep ... sleep ... sleep ...

Ingeborg sways

Not *you*, Ingeborg . . . (*To Kitty*) Sleep . . . sleep . . . sleep. . .

Lighting immediately *cross-cuts to high UR rostrum*

SCENE 10
A Road

During this scene, although unlit, Steiner, Kitty, Ingeborg and Mrs Bancroft remain frozen. During the preceding scene, the sled profile has been quietly struck. We discover D'Arcy, Otto, Bancroft and the Pastor running on the spot, as if from R to L. Bancroft carries a lantern to light the road. An effects projector projects snow on to the cyclorama through the UR arch. The sound of wind

D'Arcy Come on, Pastor! You're holding us up!

Pastor I'm sorry, I keep tripping over my rosary beads!

Bancroft Aren't you a Lutheran?

Pastor Yes, but I don't believe in taking chances!

Otto (*pointing ahead*) I can see the lights of the castle!

Bancroft Pray God we're in time!

D'Arcy No more talking! Just *run*!

Lighting immediately *cross-cuts to DL area*

SCENE 11
Walpurgisdorf Castle

Steiner still swinging the watch. Kitty is beginning to succumb

Steiner Deep . . . deep . . . Now, my dear, think of this bauble as the moon . . . The moon has a fascination for you, doesn't it?—a *horrible* fascination . . . It repels you, and yet at the same time it attracts you . . . You fight it, and yet it *calls* you . . . It *calls* you . . . The moon *calls* you . . .

A low deep growling in Kitty's throat. Ingeborg turns to look off

That's right, my dear. That's right.

Kitty howls

Excellently, my dear, excellently!

Ingeborg Herr Professor!

Steiner What is it?

Ingeborg Kommen Sie her! (*She points off through the DL entrance*)

Steiner joins her, looks off

Steiner They are returning. But they will be too late. She is coming to term. Soon, I will show her the moon, and then—(*He indicates the moon through the UL arch, and suddenly freezes, his hands holding his throat, his back to us*)

Ingeborg Herr Professor?

Steiner stumbles slowly UL, up the steps, staring up at the moon. Music starts playing again. The moon grows brighter, the moonlight now creeping and spilling into the DR area. Otto, D'Arcy, Bancroft and the Pastor have by now left the UR area

Herr Professor! Was ist los?

Steiner turns front, pulls off his rubber gloves and stares in horror at his hairy hands

Steiner No! ... Not *me*! ... Her! ... *Her!* (*He points down to Kitty, screams, clutches at his throat, falls down the steps to Kitty's L, rises, hands to face, and stumbles out DL.* Immediately, *he backs back on stage, hands still over his face—a different actor*)

Ingeborg Herr Professor? Was soll ich machen, Herr Professor?

Steiner turns to her, pulls down his hands. His face is hideous and hairy, although he still wears the little lamp in the centre of his forehead. A loud growl. Ingeborg screams

Nein! Nein!

She backs down the steps and falls. Steiner pounces on her and tears her throat out. Her terrible shriek wakes up Kitty

Kitty What is it? What's happened? (*She sees Steiner and screams*) Oh no! Not again!

Steiner goes to kill her. Mrs Bancroft struggles and chokes. Steiner looks at her, and crosses between them. He pauses, looking from one to the other, scratching his head. He doesn't know which one to kill first. He counts on his fingers, chooses Kitty and goes to her. She screams. He puts hands around her throat and—snarling horribly—bends to bite out her throat. A much louder growling and several thuds against the small door. Steiner looks across at it. With a final crash, it is smashed open, splintering, and Martin the werewolf rolls out, springs to his feet, and faces Steiner. Steiner leaves Kitty and pounces to face Martin. The two werewolves circle one another, snarling horribly, and then leap on one another. A terrible battle ensues. After a moment, D'Arcy, Otto, Bancroft and the Pastor rush on. Bancroft is still carrying his lantern

D'Arcy Good God! (*He fires his rifle again and again at the battling were-wolves, but Otto holds his arm*)

Otto You're wasting you're time! We used up all the silver bullets on those damned wolves!

Bancroft Let's get the women out of here!

He puts his lantern down on the steps, LC, and helps Otto release Mrs Bancroft. D'Arcy releases Kitty. Steiner snatches up the lantern and lifts it over his head to hurl at Martin. Martin dodges R. Steiner throws the lantern and it goes off through the DR entrance. A loud whoosh and a red glow from here. Smoke begins to filter onto the stage

D'Arcy They've set the place on fire!
Otto Never mind about that! Let's get out of here!

All stumble out DL, leaving the two werewolves to battle it out. The smoke grows thicker. Loud roaring and crackling of flames, An effects projector bathes the entire scene in leaping flames. Piano plays thundering music. Our last view of the werewolves is of both suddenly pausing in their fight and looking upwards as a loud, smashing, splintering sound is heard. They howl in terror and crouch down, arms over their heads. Fade to BLACKOUT

SCENE 12

High Ground

A continuous rumbling during the BLACKOUT. *Lighting comes up on high UR rostrum as the exhausted Otto, Bancroft, Mrs Bancroft, D'Arcy, Kitty and the Pastor stagger on from UR, come to the edge of the rostrum and stare down. The rumbling rises, and then begins to die away*

Otto The entire castle has collapsed.
Bancroft Yes ... that's the end of Konrad and his mad dreams, I'm afraid.
D'Arcy Why be afraid? It was for the best, wasn't it?

The rumbling dies. The piano plays a gentle morning sound. The light brightens. Kitty rests her head on D'Arcy's shoulder

Kitty Oh, D'Arcy!
D'Arcy It's all right, Miss Bancroft, it's all over now.
Otto Yes, look—the sun's coming out.

The scene brightens

Mrs Bancroft You've been a good servant, D'Arcy.
D'Arcy I take that as a great compliment, Madam. You'll understand why one day.
Bancroft Poor old Konrad.
Pastor Sic transit gloria mundi.
All Amen.

Crashing music on piano. Tableau. Golden light brightens around them. Fade to BLACKOUT. *Immediately restore full lighting. All come downstage, as they sing:*

SONG: **Reprise: Open Your Eyes**

All   Oh all you have to do is open your eyes
            Look at the sun
            Look at the sky

            Yes, all you have to do is use your eyes
            Look at the clouds
            Give it a try ... now

(The werewolves join the line, dancing)

> Oh all you have to do is just look around
> Isn't it fine?
> Isn't it fine?
> Isn't it grand?
> Isn't it grand?
>
> Yes, all you see is waiting there to be found
> Say that it's yours
> Hold out a hand . . . 'cause
>
> Life is never quite as bad as you think it is
> Ski-da-di-dat!
> Every day is just another great adventure
>
> But only if you always open your eyes
> Take it all in
> See where you've been

Tableau finish. If further reprises are called for, the most appropriate is Don't Sing The Words. *Otherwise, the—*

CURTAIN *falls*

FURNITURE AND PROPERTY PLOT

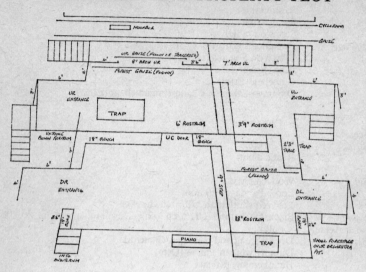

ACT I

Scene 1
Set   Moonbox in position in UR arch
Open   Grave-trap
               Wooden door in UC arch (out of sight)
Onstage   Spade (**Gravedigger**)
Offstage   Litter and lowering lines (**Pallbearers**)

Scene 2
Set   Ornate chair
Close   Grave trap
               Wooden door in UC arch
Offstage   Cases, skis and skates (**D'Arcy**)
               Toy rabbit (**Steiner**)
               Tray with three wine glasses (**Ingeborg**)
Personal   Umbrella and handbag (**Mrs Bancroft**)
               Penny whistle (**Ramsey**)
               Black glove (**Otto**)

Scene 3
Strike   Ornate chair
Set   Bed and dressings
Fly in
(or traverse) Gauze curtain in UR arch
Offstage   Stethoscope (**Steiner**)
Personal   Penny whistle (**Ramsey**)

Scene 4
Strike   Bed and dressings
Fly out
(or traverse)   Gauze curtain in UR arch
Open   Wooden door in UC arch (out of sight)
Set   Rustic table
                      Rustic chair
                      Stein (on table)
Offstage   Documents (**Otto**)
                      Tray with 5 steins (**D'Arcy**)
                      Rifle (**Ernst**)
                      Gamebag (**Ernst**)
                      Dummy of woman's hand (in gamebag) (**Ernst**)

Scene 5
Strike   Rustic table
                      Rustic chair
                      Tray with steins
Set   Wooden chair
                      Loose bandages on floor
                      Louvred shutters in UR arch (tracked)
Fly in   Black leg behind UL arch (unless cyclorama can be lit UR
(or traverse)   only)
Personal   Doctor's bag and bandages (**Bancroft**)
                      Dummy woman's hand (**Otto**)
                      Handkerchief (**Steiner**)

Scene 6
Strike   Wooden chair
                      Louvred shutters in UR arch (tracked)
Fly out
(or traverse)   Black leg in UL arch (if used)
Set   Barred cell-door in UC arch
Offstage   Penny whistle (**Steiner**)
                      2 rifles (**Sergeant**)
                      2 greatcoats (**Sergeant**)
Personal   Newspaper (**Sergeant**)
                      Whistle (**Sergeant**)

Scene 7
Strike   Barred cell-door in UC arch
Fly in
(or traverse   Forest gauzes
Offstage   Bent rifle (**Martin**)
                      Practical rifle (**D'Arcy**)
                      Rifle (**Otto**)
Special effects   Dummy of Ernst to fall at Kitty's feet
                      Swamp trap to be worked for Kitty
                      Glove puppets of white rabbits to be worked

Scene 8
Fly out
(or traverse)   Forest gauzes
Reset   Moonbox in position in UL arch
Set   Ornate chair
                     2 candelabra (practical)
Close   Wooden door in UC arch
Offstage   Tray with decanter and brandy glasses (**Ingeborg**)
                     Bill-hook (**Ramsey**)
                     Bloody shirt (**Ramsey**)
                     Shawl (**Kitty**)
Personal   Penny whistle (**Otto**)
                     Hair patches (**Martin**)
Special effects   Snowflakes blown on
                     Assist all werewolf changes

ACT II

Scene 1
Strike   Ornate chair
Reset   Moonbox in position in UR arch
Open   Wooden door in UC arch (out of sight)
Offstage   Lantern (practical) (**Steiner**)
                     Lantern (practical) (**Otto**)
                     Rifle (practical) (**D'Arcy**)
                     Rifle (**Otto**)
                     Rifle (**Bancroft**)
                     Lantern (practical) (**Ingeborg**)
                     Rabbit bone (**Ramsey**)
Personal   Umbrella (**Mrs Bancroft**)
                     Hip flask (**Otto**)
                     Silver bullets (**Otto**)

Scene 2
Offstage   Lantern (practical) (**Steiner**)
                     Lantern (practical) (**Otto**)
                     Rifle (practical) (**D'Arcy**)
                     Rifle (**Otto**)
                     Rifle (**Bancroft**)
Personal   Penny whistle (**Kitty**)

Scene 3
Set   Ornate chair
                     Decanter, glasses and special drink for Scene 5
Personal   Club (**Ingeborg**)

Scene 4
Personal   Lantern (practical) (**Otto**)
                     Rifle (practical) (**D'Arcy**)
                     Rifle (**Otto**)
                     Rifle (**Bancroft**)

Scene 5
During scene Open grave-trap
                Set blocking-up rostra

Scene 6
During scene Set operating chair
                Set instruments trolley, complete with hypodermic syringe in
                    tray
                Hand gag and rope to Ingeborg
                Assist Steiner to redress in operating gear, complete with rubber
                    gloves over werewolf hands
Personal   Lantern (practical) **(Bancroft)**
                Rifle (practical) **(D'Arcy)**
                Pistol (practical) **(Otto)**
                Rifle **(Bancroft)**
                Rifle **(Otto)**
Onstage   8 ski sticks

Scene 7
During scene Set sled profile
Scene 8
Personal   Lantern (practical) **(Bancroft)**
                Rifle (practical) **(D'Arcy)**
                Rifle **(Bancroft)**
                Rifle **(Otto)**
                Whip **(Otto)**
Special effects Work and handle wolf-head

Scene 9
During scene Strike sled profile
Personal   Fob-watch **(Steiner)**

Scene 10
Personal   Lantern (practical) **(Bancroft)**
                Rifle (practical) **(D'Arcy)**
                Rifle **(Otto)**
                Rifle **(Bancroft)**

Scene 11
Special effects Fire smoke gun

Scene 12
                No props

LIGHTING PLOT

Special Effects required: Moonbox, capable of being flown both R and L.
  Effects Projector (Flames) Effects Projector (Clouds) Effects Projector (Snow)
  (The latter two are optional, but obviously provide great colour if available)
Property fittings required: 2 candelabra, 3 lanterns

The main acting areas are the DL, UR, UL rostrum areas, and the DR to C
stage area.

ACT I

Scene 1
To open: Effect of dim moonlight in UR area. Moonbox dimly lit
          and cloud effects projector ON. Small area DR very
          dimly lit.
Cue 1   **Pastor:** "... Not for all time!"   (Page 2)
          Fade all lighting to Blackout

Scene 2
To open: Effect of early evening, all areas. Sunset effect on cyclo-
          rama
Cue 2   End of song   (Page 5)
          Begin check down, all areas
Cue 3   **Bancroft:** "... *That* isn't *him*."   (Page 7)
          Bring up special backlight through DR entrance
Cue 4   **Steiner**'s cross to **Ramsey**   (Page 7)
          Fade out special backlight in DR entrance
Cue 5   **Steiner:** "To live their fantasies ..."   (Page 9)
          Begin further check down, all areas
Cue 6   Exeunt leaving **Kitty** and **D'Arcy** alone   (Page 11)
          Build sunset effect on cyclorama
Cue 7   **D'Arcy**'s exit   (Page 12)
          Fade to Blackout

Scene 3
To open: Effect of dim moonlit interior on UR rostrum area. Moon-
          box dimly lit.
Cue 8   **Martin**'s appearance through gauze   (Page 13)
          Swell back-lighting

Scene 4
To open: Effect of sunset, exterior feel, all areas. Cloud projector
          ON.
Cue 9   End of song   (Page 21)
          Check down all areas

Cue 10   **Ernst**'s entrance   (Page 24)
             Begin further check down all areas. Slowly cheat in moon-
             box. All to be completed by Ernst's exit
Cue 11   **Martin:** ... "lit by moonlight."   (Page 25)
             Moonbox to full. Fade all other light to Blackout. Follow
             on with fade out of moonbox.

Scene 5
To open: Effect of dim interior light on UR rostrum area. No
             cyclorama or moonbox. One red special focused on
             downstage edge of UR rostrum to suggest firelight.
Cue 12   **Frau Gessler** depresses handle   (Page 27)
             Snap on moonbox and cyclorama in R area only (if not
             possible, UL arch to be covered with black leg)
Cue 13   **Otto** works handle   (Page 28)
             Snap revert
Cue 14   **Steiner**'s exit   (Page 30)
             Fade all lighting to Blackout

Scene 6
To open: Effect of dim interior DR and C. Blue special inside UR
             rostrum backlights UC arch
Cue 15   **Frau Gessler** lies on bench   (Page 31)
             Check down area DR and C. Swell blue backlight in UR
             rostrum
Cue 16   **Otto**'s entrance   (Page 31)
             Revert
Cue 17   **Steiner:** "Ramsey ..."   (Page 32)
             Fade all lighting to Blackout

Scene 7
To open: Effect of evening sunlight in forest glade all rostrum areas,
             UR, UL, DL. Green gobos. Gauzes to be lit. Cloud
             effects projector ON.
Cue 18   End of song   (Page 34)
             Check down UR and UL areas
Cue 19   **Martin**'s exit   (Page 35)
             Check down UR and UL areas further. Check down UL
             area. Follow on by cheating in moonbox at dim setting.
             Check down cyclorama and cloud effects projector.
Cue 20   Exeunt of **Otto** and **D'Arcy**   (Page 38)
             Fade all lighting to Blackout

Scene 8
To open: Effect of reasonably well-lit interior with main lighting
             DR and DL. Some lighting UR and UL. Practical can-
             delabra set. Moonbox at dim level. A red special focused
             DRC to suggest firelight.
Cue 21   **Steiner:** "It was Freud ...   (Page 41)
             Begin check down main areas
Cue 22   **D'Arcy**'s exit   (Page 44)
             Lose area UR, check down area UL, and swell moonbox

Cue 23	End of song	(Page 45)
	Check all areas to very dim setting	
Cue 24	**D'Arcy's** exit	(Page 47)
	Fade all lighting to Blackout. Follow on with houselights	

ACT II

Scene 1
To open: Effect of bright moonlight in all areas. Moonbox to full. Cloud effects projector ON.

Cue 25	Beginning of song	(Page 50)
	Build from FOH for song	
Cue 26	End of song	(Page 51)
	Lose FOH build, and check down all areas a little	
Cue 27	Exeunt leaving **Mrs Bancroft** alone	(Page 52)
	Check down UR and DL areas	
Cue 28	Exeunt of **Ramsey** and **Mrs Bancroft**	(Page 53)
	Cross-fade to Scene 2	

Scene 2
To open: Effect of dim interior of cave, DR and C. Blue special in UR rostrum at a low level.

Cue 29	Beginning of song	(Page 54)
	Build from FOH	
Cue 30	**Kitty's** exit	(Page 58)
	Slowly lose areas R and C.	
Cue 31	**Otto:** "We're right behind you."	(Page 58)
	Fade all lighting to Blackout	

Scene 3
To open: Effect of reasonably well-lit interior DR and DL. Cyclorama dimly lit. No moonbox.

Cue 32	**Martin** opens door off DL	(Page 60)
	Build blue special off DL	
Cue 33	**Steiner** closes doors off DL	(Page 61)
	Lose blue special off DL	
Cue 34	**Steiner:** "You are quite safe now . . . with me."	(Page 61)
	Fade all lighting to Blackout	

Scene 4
To open: Effect of blue moonlight on UR rostrum. Moonbox to full

| Cue 35 | **Bancroft's** exit | (Page 63) |
| | *Cross-fade to Scene 5* | |

Scene 5
To open: As Scene 3, plus moonbox to full

| Cue 36 | **Steiner's** mad laugh | (Page 67) |
| | *QUICK cross-fade to Scene 6* | |

Scene 6
To open: Effect of blue moonlight in a pool around the figures on UR rostrum. Snow projector ON UR cyclorama area only.

Cue 37   D'Arcy: "Put your heads down and *ski*!"   (Page 67)
            QUICK cross-fade to Scene 7

Scene 7
To open: Effect of reasonably well-lit interior DL only. Moonbox
            nearly at full
Cue 38   Steiner's approach to **Kitty** with syringe   (Page 69)
            QUICK cross-fade to Scene 8

Scene 8
To open: As Scene 6
Cue 39   Bancroft: "Come on! Run!"   (Page 70)
            QUICK cross-fade to Scene 9

Scene 9
To open: As Scene 7
Cue 40   Steiner: "Sleep . . . sleep . . . sleep . . ."   (Page 71)
            QUICK cross-fade to Scene 10

Scene 10
To open: As Scene 6
Cue 41   D'Arcy: "Just *run*!"   (Page 71)
            QUICK cross-fade to Scene 11

Scene 11
To open: As Scene 7
Cue 42   Steiner moves UL   (Page 72)
            Moonbox to full. Add in DR area
Cue 43   Steiner throws lantern off DR   (Page 72)
            Snap up red special off DR
Cue 44   General exeunt   (Page 73)
            Add flame effects projector
Cue 45   Visual   (Page 73)
            Fade all lighting to Blackout

Scene 12
To open: Effect of morning sunlight in UR rostrum area. Cloud
            effects projector ON.
Cue 46   All: "Amen."   (Page 73)
            Bring UR area to full
Cue 47   S.M. Cue   (Page 73)
            Fade all lighting to Blackout
Cue 48   S.M. Cue   (Page 73)
            Full up all areas for finale

EFFECTS PLOT

N.B. The plot assumes that all growling and snarling is done by actors offstage through microphones. This is much the best and most effective way of creating the required sounds on cue. Some of the howls can also be done this way.

Two tape-decks are required for this plot, since some effects mix into others.

ACT I

Scene 1

Cue 1	Opening of play	(Page 1)
	Faint wind, continuing	
Cue 2	**Pastor:** ". . . nor darkness to enshroud them . . ."	(Page 2)
	Faint wolf-howling mixes into the wind, continuing and rising to a crescendo during the speech	
Cue 3	Death of **Baron**	(Page 2)
	Cut wind	
Cue 4	**Pastor:** ". . . Not for all time!"	(Page 2)
	Short passage of loud wind and loud wolf-howling, fading	

Scene 2
No cues

Scene 3

Cue 5	Lights up on scene	(Page 13)
	Chiming clock strikes	
Cue 6	**S.M.** Cue	(Page 13)
	Creaking door	
Cue 7	**Ramsey** looks down at **Kitty**	(Page 13)
	Creaking door	
Cue 8	**Ramsey** fumbles in pocket	(Page 13)
	Creaking door	
Cue 9	**Steiner:** "Yes . . ."	(Page 13)
	Faint wolf-howl	
Cue 10	**Ramsey's** exit	(Page 13)
	Faint wolf-howl	

Scene 4

Cue 11	**Otto:** "There are only wolves in the forest?"	(Page 25)
	Faint wolf-howl	

Scene 5
No cues

Scene 6

Cue 12	As werewolf bends bars	(Page 31)
	Loud twanging of metal	

Scene 7

Cue 13	Lights up on scene	(Page 32)
	Gentle twittering birds	
Cue 14	Beginning of song	(Page 34)
	Fade out birds	
Cue 15	**Kitty:** "He's gone."	(Page 35)
	Faint cold wind, continuing	
Cue 16	**Kitty:** "Hurry up!"	(Page 35)
	Swell wind	
Cue 17	**Kitty:** "Oh, Mother!"	(Page 35)
	Swell wind further in sudden gust	
Cue 18	**Kitty** falls into bog	(Page 36)
	Loud bubbling, sucking sound mixed into wind	
Cue 19	**D'Arcy's** shot	(Page 36)
	Fade out wind	

Scene 8

Cue 20	**Mrs Bancroft** rests her head on Bancroft's shoulder	(Page 39)
	Sudden loud gust of cold wind	
Cue 21	**Steiner:** ". . . in a word—*maturity*!"	(Page 41)
	Loud wolf-howl, close	
Cue 22	**Steiner:** ". . . plant of *insanity*."	(Page 41)
	Quieter howl, close	
Cue 23	**Martin** rolls on the floor	(Page 46)
	Loud wind, building, continuing	
Cue 24	**Martin's** final entrance and howl, fully changed	(Page 46)
	Cut wind	

ACT II

Scene 1

Cue 25	**Otto:** "It is cursed."	(Page 50)
	Faint wolf-howl	
Cue 26	**Ramsey** ". . . occasional and transitory."	(Page 52)
	Faint wolf-howl	

Scene 2

Cue 27	**Werewolf's** exit UC	(Page 54)
	Grating sound of moving boulder	
Cue 28	**Kitty:** ". . . it seemed strangely familiar . . ."	(Page 54)
	Loud wolf-howl, close	
Cue 29	**Kitty** sinks to her knees	(Page 54)
	Grating sound of moving boulder	

Scene 3

Cue 30	**Martin** opens doors off DL	(Page 60)
	Cold, thin wind, continuing	
Cue 31	**Steiner** closes doors off DL	(Page 61)
	Cut wind	

Scene 4

Cue 32	Lights up on scene	(Page 61)
	Owl hooting	

Cue 33	**D'Arcy:** "... to a dead end."	(Page 61)
	Creaking sound	
Cue 34	**D'Arcy:** "I think it's loose!"	(Page 61)
	Creaking sound	
Cue 35	**D'Arcy:** "all together!"	(Page 62)
	Louder creaking sound	

Scene 5
No cues

Scene 6

Cue 36	Lights up on scene	(Page 67)
	Wind and sliding skis, continuing	
Cue 37	**Otto:** "... up my sleeve yet."	(Page 67)
	Loud wolf-howling mixes in	
Cue 38	**D'Arcy:** "Put your heads down and *ski*!"	(Page 67)
	Cut wind and sliding skis	

Scene 7
No cues

Scene 8

Cue 39	Lights up on scene	(Page 69)
	Wind, horse's hooves, sleigh-bells, continuing	
Cue 40	**Otto:** "My arm's getting tired, as it is!"	(Page 69)
	Loud wolf-howling mixes in	
Cue 41	**Bancroft:** "Look out!"	(Page 72)
	Crash of sled hitting tree mixes in, and then cut wind, horse's hooves and sleigh-bells	

Scene 9
No cues

Scene 10

Cue 42	Lights up on scene	(Page 71)
	Wind, continuing	
Cue 43	**D'Arcy:** "Just *run*!"	(Page 71)
	Cut wind	

Scene 11

Cue 44	**Steiner** throws lantern off DR	(Page 72)
	Loud whoosh of flames bursting out, and then crackle of burning timber, continuing	
Cue 45	**S.M.** Cue	(Page 73)
	Splinter and crash of collapsing ceiling mixes in, followed by rumbling of collapsing building, continuing	

Scene 12

Cue 46	All entrances complete on UR rostrum	(Page 73)
	Swell rumbling, then fade to lower level	
Cue 47	**D'Arcy:** "It was for the best, wasn't it?"	(Page 73)
	Fade out rumbling	

SPECIAL EFFECTS

The play calls for: 1 practical rifle; 1 practical pistol; 1 smoke gun

All these effects can be produced in other ways, of course, but none will be quite as dramatic.

Printed in Great Britain by Butler & Tanner Ltd, Frome and London